GOULASH
GARAGE SALES
&GOD

GOULASH
GARAGE SALES
&GOD

Bernadette McCarver Snyder

Liguori
ONE LIGUORI DRIVE
LIGUORI MO 63057-9999

Imprimi Potest:
Harry Grile, CSsR, Provincial
Denver Province, The Redemptorists

Published by Liguori Publications
Liguori, Missouri 63057

To order, call 800-325-9521
www.liguori.org

Cataloging-in-Publication Data on file with the Library of Congress

p ISBN: 978-0-7648-2369-5
e ISBN: 978-0-7648-6860-3

Some essays in this book were selected from the author's book *Mildew, Mudpies, and Miracles* (© 1995)

Liguori Publications, a nonprofit corporation, is an apostolate of The Redemptorists. To learn more about The Redemptorists, visit Redemptorists.com.

Printed in the United States of America
17 16 15 14 13 / 5 4 3 2 1
First Edition

Dedication

For all the wise and wonderful women who have touched my life gently—my mother, my sister, my teachers, my relatives, my friends. They have shown me how to look at the world and see apple pandowdy instead of crab apples. They have shown me that, no matter what comes around the corner, you can enjoy life if you welcome it with a laugh and a prayer.

Contents

Introduction

A re you near the end of your rope and fresh out of cope? Is your life like a sweater with little fuzzies all over it? When you try to make it better by pulling a loose thread, does the whole thing start to unravel? I know how you feel.

As you thumb through this book, you will read all about my fuzzies and loose threads. You will also notice that this book wanders—just like my mind. Words written at the end of a rope do not always fall in sequence. These are just wanderings that I have dashed down through the years.

The famous author Edith Wharton once wrote something that I remember but may be quoting loosely. Her idea was that a woman's nature is like a great house full of rooms. There's the hall, through which everyone passes, going in and out, and the drawing room, where one receives formal visits, and the sitting room, where members of the family gather, coming and going through the years. But beyond that, far beyond, there are other rooms, the handles of whose doors perhaps are seldom turned.

As you and I "turn the handles" in this book, I hope you will enjoy and maybe identify with the goulash of life that can be mixed-up but delicious, the fun of finding treasures in garages or wherever you least expect them, and of course, the warm, welcoming grace of God everywhere.

Please note: Some of the meanderings in this book may have appeared earlier in books now out of print. If you find one you've read before, I hope you will enjoy it the second time around.

A Touch of Magic

When I was a little kid, there was a "magic place" in my grandma's backyard. It was just a little shady spot between the foundation of the house and a large overhanging flowery bush—just big enough for a small person to crawl into and be hidden from the outside world. I used to go there—sometimes alone, sometimes with a playmate—and in that "secret garden" I could travel to exotic places, to lands of adventure and discovery, intrigue and excitement. And it didn't take any money or advance scheduling. All it took was imagination.

When I grew up and got lost in the world of work and worry, I almost forgot the magic of withdrawing to a quiet place to dream, to plan, to drink in the beauty of the moment, to pray, and to just "be." But then my son came along.

Although he was busily into everything and usually kept me chasing after him, there would be times when I would look out my kitchen window and see him in the backyard—in his little log-cabin playhouse, arms crossed on the windowsill, just staring off into space. Other times, I would see him, all alone, lying flat on his back in the grass, gazing at the clouds, totally oblivious to all around him. And I knew he was journeying into imagination, as I had done so many years before. I knew he had found the magic.

Dear Lord, I've tried to hang on to the "secret garden" my son helped me recapture. When I get caught in the quicksand, I remind myself to reach out for that flowered branch that can pull me into a journey of dreams or back to the safety of quiet prayer and meditation and peace. I am so grateful, Lord, that you gave me this magic gift of imagination. How sad that some of today's children—and adults—are always hurrying to pre-scheduled games, club meetings, and activities, or sitting in front of a TV screen, watching the results of the imagination of someone *else*. Help us, Lord. Don't let us lose the magic.

The Closet Caper

I'm so excited. I just learned that my son's closet has been declared a historic landmark!

Oh, I don't mean his current closet—the one with all the baseball cards and the tennis shoes that smell prehistoric and the nice ties he's never worn and the good suit he outgrew two years ago and the cage for the gerbil that died three years ago. No, that closet could only be declared fit for a city landfill.

The historic closet is in an apartment building where we lived when I was first married. That was our first home, and it was full of challenges. The living room was long and skinny, and I spent a year rearranging the furniture, sure that I would find a way to make it look fatter and friendlier. I never did.

But the biggest conversation piece was always the hall closet. That closet was bigger than the kitchen and about half as big as our bedroom—and it had two doors, which made it the only room in the apartment that had cross-ventilation!

The second year we lived there, our son was born, and it only seemed logical to turn such a "choice" location into his nursery.

We painted it and decorated it and moved in a chest of drawers and a crib and a fluffy white music-box lamb that played a lullaby. All our friends were either amused or aghast. We were the only ones with a kid in a closet.

But he lived happily there until we saved enough money to move into a small house where he could have a real room of his own.

Through the years, I would occasionally drive by to take a nostalgic look at our former home, but it began to deteriorate. One day, I drove past and saw that it was empty with the windows boarded up and all the beautiful flower beds long gone. It was like running into an old friend who has fallen upon hard times.

I grieved a bit and would remember the happy times we spent there when I looked through the old photo album.

And then, today there was this big article in the newspaper with a photo of the building as I remembered it, announcing that this "historic landmark" is to be rehabbed and reborn.

I don't know why they called it "historic" unless someone told them about our nursery closet, but I'm happy to know that soon some new families will come along and enjoy its old-world charm and its cross-ventilated closet!

Dear Lord, thank you for all the joyful times in that old building. We had so little money in those days—but so much fun and so much hope for the future. Please help all the couples just starting out today, Lord—especially the ones who might think you have to start with a big beautiful new house, two new cars, and enough money for fancy vacations. And remind me again, Lord, to appreciate all the small blessings in my life and remember that I don't need lots of things to make a closet full of memories.

Here's Mud in Your Pie—and Your Ear and Your Toes and...

Pies are big in our house, just like Mom used to make—peach, apple, cherry, and *mud*. Yes, the most popular pies at our house were mud. My son had a love-at-first-sight relationship with mud. He saw it, he jumped into it, he bonded with it. And then I made the mistake of showing him how to make mud pies.

Actually, I probably didn't have to show him. He would have learned on his own. He and mud stuck together as tightly as a department-store price label on a sale item you planned to give as a gift. And pies were not his only specialty. There was bucket o' mud, mug o' mud, face o' mud.

Instead of a backyard sandbox, we had a mud hole. I hated sand, so one day when the yard was soft after a rain, I pounded in four sturdy planks to make a box. Then I told my son and his friends if they would leave the rest of the yard alone, they could dig in this dirt box all they wanted to. And they wanted to! They spent many happy hours there, creating mud monsters, mud mountains, and mud to clog Mother's washing machine.

Some houses have mud rooms. Ours had a mud garage. And we had a rule. Before my son entered the house, I would hose him off and then make him step into the garage and out of his clothes. One day he forgot the hosing-off step and just dropped his clothes and ran into the house with face, hands, and feet still covered with mud, but the once-clothed parts now uncovered. This created quite a stir since that was the day I was serving tea and cookies to company. That day my son and I *did* serve up a surprise—a "mud pie moment" our visitors never forgot.

Dear Lord, thank you for mud and memories. Without mud, how could we have flowers, grassy lawns, or photo albums with pictures of a little boy whose sparkly eyes and happy, gap-toothed grin are shining through that muddy face? Help parents—and all of us—Lord, to be aware that the kind of dirt that washes out is not so bad for children.

It's the kind of dirt that gets dished out all-too-freely today on TV, in movies, magazines, and videos. *That* dirt can cause permanent damage and soil an attitude and a life forever.

Help us, Lord, to recognize that kind of dirt before it gets "ground in" and accepted as a part of everyday life. Help us, Lord, to avoid mud pies of the mind and tolerate only *your* kind of mud—the kind that makes good gardens grow, the kind that is dug up by happy little boys and little girls in backyard mud puddles.

Tell Your Lilac
to Go Play in Traffic!

This year, I discovered one of the secrets of the Green Thumb Club: Lilacs like traffic.

Horticulturists may disagree, but I have proof. It all began several years ago when I carefully planted a lilac bush in what I considered a perfect spot in my backyard. It grew into a large green plant—which was nice—but what I wanted were those lacy, sweet-smelling lilac flowers that perfume the springtime.

Friends kept telling me that it takes a long time for lilacs to bloom and to wait and be patient. I was patient for eight years.

When we moved to a new house, I almost went off and left the lilac in the lurch, but finally I dug it up and dragged it along. In its new backyard, it grew again into a bush with no flowers.

Two years later, a big evergreen out front died, and when we dug it out there was a nice big hole—ready to be filled. I didn't have another bush on hand, and the lilac was in the backyard where another hole wouldn't matter, so we transplanted it again.

It was a bad day for transplanting—hot and dry. My son and I started out digging carefully, trying not to break the roots—but the hotter it got, the faster we dug. Finally, we yanked out the roots, dumped them in the hole, and hoped for the best.

Obviously, I had been too polite to that lilac in the past because the next spring what had been a nice green bush all those years turned into a nice green bush with *two* blossoms!

When I saw the blooms, I ran into the house screaming and shouting about something wonderful happening. My husband thought we must have won a million-dollar lottery. He was just a *little* disappointed when I told him about the two lilac blooms.

But the best was yet to come. This spring, the lilac bush was absolutely covered with fragrant flowers, just as a lilac bush is supposed to be. And there could be only one explanation—lilacs like traffic.

All those years the lilac had been in a backyard. When I finally moved it to the front, right by the side of the garage where it could watch the traffic and inhale the gas fumes, it choked, gasped, and bloomed!

✠

Dear Lord, that lilac reminds me of children. Sometimes we expect them to grow in the backyard of our life, with just an occasional pat on the head and a birthday hug. And many do just fine that way. But other children need a little extra. Like the lilac, they just can't seem to bloom where they were planted. They need a different kind of atmosphere, attention, or situation.

Sometimes a parent has to keep "moving them about," tugging at their roots, putting them in a different school or activity, suggesting new projects or possibilities to help them find a bloom-able spot in life. The secret—as with most things—is patience, endurance, and paying attention. If one thing doesn't work, try another. Never give up. That's the way you treated me, isn't it, Lord? You've tugged at my roots a lot. I was a late bloomer, but you never gave up on me. Thank you, Lord, for paying attention.

Just a Taste

There is no accounting for some people's tastes! That's one of the basic facts I learned at my mother's knee. But I didn't know the same was true with animals until we got a dog who ate green apples and ice cubes.

That dog was always so close on the heels of my son and his friends that he thought he was "one of the boys," so naturally he ate what they ate. When I handed out green apples, he expected one, too. And when he saw the boys bite into theirs, he settled down to gnaw dutifully, just like his buddies. In the summer, when I ran out of Popsicles, the boys had to settle for ice cubes, and the dog learned to beg for those, too. The worst was the first time I opened a can of chili after the dog had come to live at our house. The minute that aroma hit the air, the dog came to attention, looking longingly at the stove and giving me the poor-pitiful-little-hungry-me look. Up until that moment, I had had no reason to suspect that dog had Mexican ancestry.

When I sat down to eat the chili, his eyes followed every spoonful I lifted. Before long, we were both in a terrible emotional state! He was shaking and whimpering so much that I was afraid he was going to start a Mexican hat dance. Finally, I decided to put a spoonful of chili into his bowl, sure that the first fiery bite would discourage him. I was wrong. He loved the taste so much, he gave new meaning to the phrase, "Give it a licking."

A few days later, I opened a carton of raspberry yogurt. Suddenly, the dog's gourmet nose went into action again. Since yogurt does not exactly smell like chili, I thought his nose had misfired. To show him he had made a mistake, I put a spoonful of yogurt into his dish. He lapped up every drop.

Well, I suppose it was inevitable for us to get a dog who has strange tastes—like everybody else in the family. My son likes fried okra. When I serve that, my husband acts like we're trying to poison him if we even let the bowl of okra come near his end of the table. But my husband likes cornmeal mush and puts pepper on sweet potatoes. And I am the one who indulgently puts up with my husband, my son, and the dog. There is just no accounting for some people's tastes!

Dear Lord, you must have had a lot of fun making people—and animals—with such different tastes! Some casual acquaintances will rush in your front door and give you a big hug. Some lifelong friends act like a handshake is an invasion of privacy. Some people will go to church and sing out loud, sing out strong—whether they know how to sing or not. Others will never warble a note. And let's not even think about the differences people have when you start talking about art or politics or the best spaghetti recipe. Lord, thank you for putting so many strange tastes in your world. It just wouldn't have been as delicious without all the differences.

Finding the Fountain of Youth

Next Sunday, I think I'll wear my bathing cap to church! In fact, I may start wearing that swim cap wherever I go.

You see, I was lucky enough to go swimming in an indoor pool in the middle of winter. That was wonderful, but I knew it would be a bit chillier than in the summer, and I am one of those people who is only warm enough when the temperature hits "stifling." So I decided I would unearth my old swim cap and wear that to keep my head warm.

After a few minutes of my amateurish type of swimming—which takes a lot of energy and a lot of nerve—I warmed up enough to enjoy the refreshing exercise. But later, in the dressing room as I was trying to stuff my damp body into dry clothes, I noticed that my head was the only area that was comfortably warm.

Since swim caps never keep my hair totally dry, I knew the minute I took off the cap, my wet hair would set off a freeze alert and send my body into the sneeze-sniffle pattern. So I decided to drive home wearing the swim cap.

The pool is just a few blocks from my house, and I knew that as soon as I got home, I could stick my wet head under a warm hair dryer. But as I was driving along, getting double-takes from every car I passed, I happened to glance in the visor mirror.

I was amazed to see that the cap had wrought a miracle!

True, I looked weird—but I also looked wrinkle-less. The cap fit so tight, it had pulled all the wrinkles off my face! I guess it worked just like those expensive face-lifts where the doctor takes "tucks" at your temples to empty the bags under your eyes.

Well, of course as soon as I took off my cap, the wrinkles returned. And it became obvious that the only way I could make time stand still would be to wear this swim cap wherever I go.

Dear Lord, isn't it strange how we have all gotten to the point where we will go to any lengths to look young—even if we also look ridiculous? We think young is best, young is beautiful, young is where the action is, young is irresistible. Actually, young is fleeting and irretrievable.

When I was young, old was beautiful and revered and honored. But, as usual, my timing was bad and I started getting "mature" at the wrong time. Oh well, why should I worry? At least, Lord, *you* still love old as much as young. Thank you for that, Lord. Thank you for loving me as I am—with or without a swim cap.

My Purse on Wheels

If you are judged by the car you keep, I am in a no-parking zone on the highway of life. A friend once took a look in my car and said, "The inside of your car is so full of stuff, it looks like a purse on wheels."

Yep, that's my car—a purse on wheels.

My husband is afraid to ride in my car—not because he thinks I'm an unsafe driver but because he's afraid he won't be able to find a seat. But some friends *like* to ride with me because their cars look the same and seeing mine makes them feel less guilty.

Actually, I'm not really messy, just prepared. One snowy day, I looked in the back seat and observed snow boots, an umbrella, a hat, gloves, a coat hanger, a small American flag, and a book. I explained that to myself by rationalizing that in case of emergency, I could wave the flag to try to attract attention or I could just sit and read the book until help arrived. If help did not arrive, I could put on my warm hat, gloves, and boots and take my umbrella and coat hanger for protection and wade through the snow to go seek help.

My rationalization became prophetic. Two days later, the emergency arrived. As I was hurtling along in the fast lane as usual, my car got tired. It turned off its motor to take a nap. Luckily, I managed to coast almost off the road and my car ended up partly on the shoulder and partly in danger of being smashed to smithereens by oncoming traffic at any moment.

I fumbled through the stuff in my purse and found the cell phone but *of course* this was one of those days when I forgot to recharge it, so it also was napping. So I put on my hat and gloves to keep warm, but I decided it was snowing too hard for anyone to see me waving the flag, and I couldn't relax quite enough to read the book.

Instead, I read the owner's manual that had been in the glove compartment, untouched for many moons. It had nothing to suggest for a car napping on a snowy shoulder.

I was just about to reach for the boots, umbrella, and coat hanger when a police car came. The officer's phone was awake, so he called a tow truck, which hauled me to the nearest little countryside gas station. The local yokels opened the hood, peered in, shook their heads, and began to whistle "Taps." Since the tow truck driver was still inside the station drinking coffee, he agreed to tow me—at great cost—to my friendly neighborhood garage, where I am known. They have seen my pitiful pleading act before, so they agreed to bring my car back to life.

While it was being rehabilitated, I began to realize how dependent I was on this four-wheeled wonder. How did women of past generations manage to raise children, run errands, keep house, and keep their sanity without auto-mation? How did Cleopatra ever set styles on the Nile with only a chauffeur-driven barge? How did Madame Curie ever discover anything when she had to take a horse or a trolley to the laboratory? How did our grandmothers survive without a purse on wheels?

Dear Lord, every day I hit the highways and byways, list in hand, confident that I know where I'm going and how to get there. But when I hit a detour or have a breakdown, I realize I'm not really in control. Remind me, Lord, not to be too dependent on things or routines. I should only be dependent on you. So thank you, Lord, for my purse on wheels. Ride with me and help me remember that I am the traveler but *you* are in the driver's seat.

It Was a Cat-astrophe!

The fur has been flying at our house recently. Everywhere I look, I spot little golden blobs—not of money but of fur. I am beginning to suspect that my cat has read the story about kids leaving a trail of bread crumbs to find the way home. Since the weather got warm, he has been leaving a trail of yellow fur wherever he goes—so now *anybody* could find the way to my house.

Maybe leopards can't change their spots or tigers their stripes, but this cat has sure been changing his coat—and leaving pieces of it all over the neighborhood. Actually, I guess it's natural for someone who's been wearing a fat yellow-fur coat all winter to feel the need to shed it for the summer. I just wish he wouldn't shed it on my good slacks.

Actually, I'm glad there's a change-of-weather explanation for his change of fur. Otherwise, I might be expected to take him to a cat psychologist to find out why he's acting this way. The other day I read about a lady who had to consult a pet psychologist to find out why her usually well-behaved pet had changed. The doctor told her it was because she wasn't spending enough "quality time" with the pet. Expert or no, when I have any quality time to spend, it's not going to be spent with the cat!

Today the idea of "quality time" has become a catch phrase, a cure-all for many problems. Some husbands, wives, parents, and children think they can be too busy for each other most of the time—and then make up for their apartness by occasionally spending an hour of quality time together.

Our world has become work-weary, too busy to *be*. If we're too busy to find time for each other, then we're surely too busy to find time for prayer. The other day I went to a seminar where it was suggested you should find two twenty-minute times each day to just sit quietly and put yourself in the presence of God. Many in the audience (including me) began to think how we spend more than twenty-minute segments each day to fret, fume, criticize, or clean up cat fur. Maybe we've been forgetting how important it is to leave a trail of prayer, thoughtfulness, and togetherness—so we can find our way home.

Dear Lord, here I am saying "I'm sorry" again. But I am. I know I should spend more time in quiet prayer with you. Thank you for listening, Lord. Stay with me, and help me to make it through every busy day so that I won't just leave a trail of crumbs but a trail of something more substantial, more lasting, more loving. And, Lord, could you *please* help that cat get rid of his coat so he and I both can stop worrying about the de-furring and get back to our purring.

The Greening
of America

The grass is always greener, not just on the other side of the fence, but also when it's growing between the bricks in the walkway, between the cracks in the concrete driveway, and right in the middle of my flower bed!

Ignoring that fact, every spring I embark on the heartbreaking—and backbreaking—adventure of trying to make my lawn look like bright green indoor-outdoor carpeting. And I am not alone. The whole neighborhood is out there, weeding, seeding, dethatching, and following the instructions for "ground enrichment." And what do we get for all our troubles and the de-enrichment of our budgets? The prospect of spending all those lazy, crazy days of summer with a lawn mower cutting down what we have encouraged to grow up!

This preoccupation with the lawn seems to fit in with our society's well-publicized love for the green. But maybe growing green grass is worth it after all. In my "scientific" research, I have learned that an acre of grass is like a seventy-ton air conditioner that returns 2,400 gallons of water to the atmosphere on a sunny day. Most of us don't have a whole acre to cultivate, but even a twenty-foot-square plot of grass supplies enough oxygen to keep an adult breathing. Isn't that amazing? I'll try to remember that the next time I'm out there, mowing, groaning, and gasping for breath.

But there's more good news. It seems that, if combed out, a 2,500-square-foot lawn would contain about 482 million separate plants. I don't know who spent time combing out a lawn to discover that, but it *is* reassuring to know that all those millions of plants are busily pumping clean air and water into our atmosphere almost as fast as people are pumping pollution into it!

I'm going to meditate on that tomorrow, but right now I've gotta get out there and pull out those oxygen-pumpers that are growing between the bricks, in the concrete cracks, and all over my flower garden!

Dear Lord, have you noticed how some folks are like a lawn? Some never green up, no matter how much feeding and care, cultivating and enhancing they get. They are the brown-and-downers, always blaming their brownness on something that happened in the past, when they were growing up. Other people are the sunny-side-ups, growing and flourishing in spite of the fact that they never got enough attention or enrichment, determined to reach for the light even when days are cloudy.

Lord, help us remember that no matter how our "roots" were fertilized as we were growing up, it is never too late to grow out of it. Unlike computers, humans can reprogram themselves if they really truly want to do it. Lord, if you gave tiny blades of grass the power to pump clean air and water into a polluted atmosphere, what far greater power have you given us humans? Thank you, Lord, thank you.

It's a Mystery!

"Who done it?" is a popular phrase at our house—and not just when a dish gets broken or a secret gets spilled. Instead of trying to avoid that question, we frequently try to outwit each other so we can be the first to answer it—because we love mystery stories!

My husband started it—like he starts lots of things! He is a longtime mystery fan, and his favorite music is the soundtrack from that old movie *How to Murder Your Wife*. (I hope it's just the music he likes and not the plot of the movie.)

When we were first married, I couldn't understand why he wasted his time reading junky mysteries. Then I landed in the hospital for a few days and, instead of bringing me flowers or candy, my beloved brought me a paperback murder mystery. When I opened the package, I wanted to murder *him*!

But being the wonderful person that I am—and having absolutely nothing else to do—I read the book. It was the best medicine he could have brought me! I didn't have time to think about aches, pains, or the hospital heebie-jeebies. I was too busy reading as fast as I could, trying to figure out "who done it."

After that, I understood and shared my husband's mysterious reading habit. Now we both enjoy mystery books, movies, and TV shows. Maybe we like them so much because when we were growing up, there wasn't much mystery in our lives.

His youth was pretty much like mine. My parents watched every move I made, told me what to do and not to do, where I could go and where I couldn't go, and exactly what time I was expected to get home. I hated it.

They also let me know they loved me and complimented me when I did anything right and bragged on me to their friends. I hated that, too. I was embarrassed to overhear them talking about me.

Maybe because of their protective smothering, I was a late bloomer. It took me a while to grow up. And I've been grateful ever since. I've enjoyed being an independent adult, but I'm glad I didn't miss that time when I was a protected, loved child.

Dear Lord, today's psychology tells parents to leave the kids alone, let them make their own decisions, do their own thing. We parents are told we should be free to live our own lives instead of spending so much time caring for or helping our children. I'm sure all this must be very wise and right for some—but I'm grateful my parents never heard about it!

Lord, help today's parents know how to hold tight with open hands. Help us to teach our children that freedom must be balanced by some basic rules and commandments. Help us to show them that loving dependence can take some of the fear out of independence. And help us to find the time to enjoy sharing those youthful years. All too soon, babies grow into independent adults, and parents wonder where the years and the opportunities went. It's a mystery.

Put a Cork in It!

I've always known my husband was a corker, but this week he proved it. He announced he would like my help in corking a wall. That sounded like a good idea. I agreed.

It was *not* a good idea. It was the kind of ordeal that, once you survive it, you know nothing else could be worse. You know that if you have lived through that, then you will never ever have to worry about divorce court. The family that corks together stays together.

Actually, you are stuck with each other in more ways than one! You see, the only way to apply this cork to a wall is with an awful, tar-looking substance that's a lifetime glue. It's so thick you have to use a trowel to dig it out of the can. Then you sort of hurl this black stuff toward the wall and try to quickly smear it around without spilling any on anything. I spilled it on everything.

From that moment on, we really were "stuck" together. We had glue stuck on our clothes, in our hair, on our hands, and in our shoes. Glue was on everything except the cat—and that's only because he was smarter than we were. He took one look at the situation and headed for his nearest hideout.

Oh well, it might not have been a fun experience, but it sure was an exciting one—all that shouting at each other, words and glue flying through the air, insults and cork being flung about, hammers and harangues dropped, tacks and tempers lost.

It was well worth the trouble, though, when we ended up with this bright, spanking-new, cork-covered wall—interestingly decorated here and there with big black smudges of leftover glue. Luckily, my husband had plans for that wall and has already covered the whole thing with pinned-on maps. Now only we, the perpetrators, know about the dark smudges that lie hidden—like so many family secrets—beneath the corking bright veneer seen by outsiders.

Dear Lord, I guess most families have some smudges like that, known only to a select few. Whenever you start digging up a family tree or paging through the past, you usually find a few black marks, a shady story here, a dark whisper of doubt there. But Lord, I know that doesn't excuse it or make it right. Every time I pass that wall, I feel a twinge of guilt. Maybe we could have done better. Maybe we should have planned ahead—or something drastic like that. And certainly we could have given our vocal cords less exercise.

Forgive us our tempers, Lord. But at least we learned a valuable lesson. Some people can design skyscrapers or build space rockets. We can't. Some people can wallpaper and lay carpet and cork walls. We can't. We've learned, Lord, that it's important to recognize our limitations. Help us to accept that—and remember that! Please, Lord, don't let us ever even think about corking a wall again!

The Muddle-Aged Mutant Unhinged Turtle

As I went to the neighborhood swimming pool for a quick dip, I finally figured out the secret reason that life today is so "weighty." It's because we have all become turtles!

I don't mean slow like turtles. Some of us in this current society move so swiftly we move ourselves right into heart attacks, stress attacks, breakdowns, and the heartbreak of bitten fingernails.

The reason we're turtle-like is because we take our "house" with us wherever we go. But I didn't realize this until that trip to the pool.

Since I was going swimming, I naturally took along a swimsuit, a towel, flip-flops, and my ridiculous-looking nose clip. But then—just in case—I also took suntan lotion, moisturizer, sunglasses, sun visor, a book and a newspaper (just in case there was no one there to visit with), an apple (just in case I got hungry), my coin purse (just in case I got thirsty for a diet cola from the soft-drink machine), and my drivers license (just in case I got stopped by a policeman while motoring the six blocks to the pool).

As I was dragging all this stuff along with me from the car, a little boy arrived to swim. He was walking along, barefoot, wearing his swimsuit and carrying a towel—period. That was it. That's all he needed to enjoy his dip. I looked at all my appendages and appurtenances and realized I had become a turtle.

Then I began to think about how often we do this. When we go on vacation, we take half the house with us. If there's anything we might need—just in case—we don't leave home without it. Even when we go on a picnic, a camping trip, or a weekend outing to get away from it all, we can't get away because we take it all with us!

Maybe that's why our society has become anxious, overburdened, troubled, and insecure today. Maybe our turtle-like ways are robbing us of God's special gift of time. Maybe we have so many things to worry about and care for that there's too little time left to smell the flowers, hear the music, soar with the eagles, and appreciate the beautiful world and beautiful people around us. Maybe we've become muddle-aged mutant unhinged turtles!

Dear Lord, I have observed a turtle up close—as many mothers have had to do when a small person appeared in the kitchen carrying a shell-covered reptile, saying, "Isn't he beautiful, Mom? Can we keep him, pulllleeeaaassse?" I have noticed that turtles must be anxious and insecure because they are always darting their heads back inside their shells to hide. And they must be overburdened carrying those heavy houses around all the time. I don't know if there are "troubled" turtles because that's another of their problems—they don't communicate too well.

Lord, I have also noticed that all this "carrying" I do has made my neck muscles tense and my shoulders sag, and I communicate often but not always well. Help me, Lord, to stop hurrying and scurrying, to come out of my shell and look up and out instead of always in. Help me to change from a turtle to a turtledove. And the next time I decide to get away from it all, remind me to leave my house at home!

Watch Out!

Time stood still this week. My watch broke. Actually, it wasn't even the watch—just the watchband. But I soon found out that a watch on the wrist is worth two in the pocket.

Since I never knew what time it was, I didn't know if I was running early or late. It was late. I didn't know if I had more time than I thought to finish something or less time. It was less. I didn't know if I should hurry or take my time. I should have hurried.

I found out that—even without a watch to alert you—time marches on. One day I sat and chatted with a friend over coffee because I was sure I had plenty of time left to get my shopping done. I didn't. I drove leisurely through traffic instead of fuming and fussing about every driver that got in my way because I was sure I had time to get to an appointment. I was wrong.

But all week, I had this euphoric feeling that I needn't hurry or scurry or even worry. Without a watch to warn me, I had no idea that I was running a day late and a dollar short all week. But you know what? By the end of the week, everything got done someway anyway.

Maybe I just won't get that watchband fixed after all. It was a lot nicer to give my friend my undivided attention and offer sympathy and empathy for her troubles and woes without always glancing at my watch, wishing she'd talk a little faster.

It was a lot nicer not to be honking my horn and darting dirty looks at other drivers. It was a lot nicer for my blood pressure to keep on an even keel instead of pushing it to its boiling point, worrying about every minute wasted.

I'm always thinking or saying, "I just don't have enough time." But I do. I have all the time there is. I have from sunrise to sunrise, summer, fall, winter, and spring. Time is not on my hands but it is *in* my hands.

Dear Lord, I think my problem is that I think I have to do everything and be everywhere every day—to make more money and more friends and more plans, to get more involved and more concerned and more indispensable. What have I been thinking, Lord? I should know that all I really have to do is your work.

Why is it, Lord, that I can manage to get up earlier in the morning to get to an appointment but not to spend time reading the Bible? Why is it I can somehow find time to get to the new movie I really want to see but can't always make it to evening church services? Why is it I can always find a little extra time to go to a party, watch a favorite TV show, or even read a book-of-the-month but can't find extra time for prayer?

Forgive me, Lord. You gave me this insatiable interest in everything and everybody, so I know you understand. I promise to find more time for quiet time with you. But Lord, you and I both know that even when there is no quiet time, you are still always with me—at the party, the picnic, the movie, the mall. And don't we have fun, Lord?

We've Been Branded!

M y son has led me astray—again. A spoonful at a time.
Our house has been rated X because I usually buy Brand X—or whatever is on sale at the supermarket each week. So for years, our freezer has known nothing but Brand X ice cream.

But one day, the son and heir had to go and eat at somebody else's house—somebody who could afford name-brand ice cream. Not just any name brand either, but the most expensive kind—the kind with no artificial ingredients, no artificial preservatives, and no half-price sales.

He came home and announced that he never wanted Brand X to pass his lips again. He had tasted the forbidden fruit and wanted more. I explained that my Brand X budget could not afford his newly acquired taste. He countered, saying he would promise to eat only half as much ice cream if I would promise to buy the expensive kind—and that would balance the budget. This sounded logical, and I've never been able to deal with logic, so I agreed.

I started buying him the "good" ice cream, and he rationed it out while his father and I pigged out on the greasy kid kind of frozen calories. But one day, in a fit of wild abandon, I tasted the expensive brand. And I liked it.

Soon I was sneaking a spoonful here, a bowlful there. And now Brand X didn't taste so good any more. I wanted the good stuff. Then my husband caught me indulging one day and asked for a taste. Now *he* had been corrupted. Our house has gone from Brand X to X-pensive. And our budget is X-hausted.

Dear Lord, I guess eating up the frozen assets is not too bad, but it could lead to worse. Have you noticed how often that happens today?

You can live in a small house for years, but as soon as you move into a larger house, you can't imagine how *anyone* could be happy living in a little dinky one. Someone gives you an expensive sweater and suddenly your old ones look tacky because they don't have a "good" label sewed in the back! You can finally afford to buy a new car and soon you start to wonder why your neighbor is satisfied driving that old junker (which looks a lot like the one you just traded in).

It's so easy today to get spoiled, Lord, to become accustomed to little luxuries and decide Brand X isn't good enough any more. Yes, Lord, I know I don't have to feel guilty about an occasional luxury, and there's nothing wrong in being satisfied to have half as much of something expensive as twice as much of something cheap. Just help me to be grateful for whatever I have, Lord, even when the budget says it has to be Brand X. And thank you, Lord, for giving me so many X-tra helpings of joy and wonder and happy X-pectations!

The Rain Came Down—and Took Me With It!

I've been in the gutter again. The rains came, the gutter over-floweth, and no one was home but me.

Just because all those raindrops couldn't fit into a clogged gutter, they splashed over into a pool at the bottom. Then, instead of staying there like good little raindrops, waiting their turn to soak into the lawn, they had to go adventuring.

They must have been very determined because they wandered around until they managed to find one tiny little crack in the foundation of our house and seeped their way into the basement. I don't know how they got in there, but I had a terrible time getting the damp things out!

I mopped. I wiped. I fumed. I fussed. I turned my hair dryer loose on the wet carpet and it blew its little motor out, but the rug remained soggy and saggy. Finally, when I had dried up everything as much as possible, I surfaced and returned to the upper part of the house. My spirits remained in the downer.

By now, the rain had stopped and I should have grabbed that chance to get out the ladder, climb up, and unclog the gutter. Instead, I grabbed a cup of coffee and the opportunity to sit down and feel sorry for myself. That's when the rain started again, the gutter overfloweth again—and so did my tear ducts.

Dear Lord, have you noticed how much better I am at crying than vying? If I had unclogged that gutter when I had the chance, I could have avoided the second cleanup. Why do I spend so much time worrying about, and feeling guilty about, all the things I could and should be doing—instead of just doing them? Please help me remember how good it feels when a hard job is finally finished, off the chore list, and on the "done" list.

Help me to clean out my clogged gutter of "later, some day, soon" and get into the free-flowing spirit of *now*! *This* is the day the Lord has made—let me rejoice and be glad and get my get-up-and-go unclogged.

No More Empty Pockets

I just read a story about a famous artist, and it gave me a great new decorating idea. It seems this genius was as handy with a hammer as he was with an artist's palette, so he decided to build himself an art studio.

Just as he finished, he realized he had forgotten to include a shelf where he could keep liquid refreshment for those long hot hours with the paint pots. Being inventive, he grabbed up an old pair of many-pocketed coveralls from the floor and plastered them into a wall, pocket-side out. When the plaster dried, he stuck some bottles of his favorite soft drink into the pockets and was ready to be refreshed.

Now why didn't I think of that?

There are several pairs of my son's old jeans I would like to plaster into a wall or stuff into the garbage can or bury in the backyard. Of course, I don't have an art studio, so it would be hard to decide which room of a subdivision house would look best decorated with the pockets of plastered pants.

It would be handy to reach for a sparkly soda or a tangy lemonade as I stoop and scrub, droop and dust—but I'd still have to go to the kitchen for ice and a glass because I'm not artistic enough to "suffer" and do without those. I guess my house and I will have to stay just the way we always are—with empty pockets.

Dear Lord, I read something else today, too—by a famous philosopher, Nietzsche. He said, "When one has much to put into them, a day has a hundred pockets." I have much to put into a day, Lord—washing dishes, cooking, running errands, reading, writing, giggling, singing, talking to a friend, feeling your nearness. Those may not be the kinds of things Nietzsche had in mind, Lord, but I'm grateful for them all. Thank you, Lord, for giving me such full days. My pockets may not have much money in them, but they are full of blessings.

The Auto
That Oughta!

I've seen TV commercials recently that show an automobile that has been programmed to park itself at the curb. I really could use one of those. Instead my old car programs itself to immediately turn in anywhere that a garage-sale sign appears. Since that car and I have been traveling together for many miles, it oughta know by now that I have a very low threshold for sales resistance, but no, it keeps turning in. And of course, I hardly ever leave a garage without a new treasure. So it's all my car's fault that my home is filled with knickknacks and what-is-its. Some have been recycled through the years, but some I still love enough to not say goodbye.

My favorite—and the one people always exclaim over—is not one of the tiny treasures. It's big enough to take up half of my marble-top table and it's hard to describe. Imagine a china figure of a young man on a horse. He's wearing a once-upon-a-time soldier's uniform and a helmet with a cross on the front. Standing beside the horse is a young lady wearing a flowing pink-flowered dress. She is reaching up to the soldier, who is bending down to kiss her goodbye. And the horse, obviously embarrassed, is looking away.

When I look at this china couple, although I've never had a flowing pink-flowered dress, I sentimentally think of the many times I've sent my husband off to do battle—not in a war, thank goodness, but with a desk full of papers waiting at his office.

Of course, I never would have had this treasure if my car had not swerved off the road when I was dashing to work early one morning. I knew I shouldn't stop at that garage sale, but my car knew better. The minute I saw this one-of-a-kind what-is-it, I knew it was *mine*.

People sometimes talk about what they would save if they ever had to evacuate their home. I know I would grab the family photo albums with one arm, but the other arm would be wrapped around my sentimental off-to-work couple.

Dear Lord, as I think about it, I believe my oughta-auto has been reprogramming itself recently. Instead of turning into garage sales, it seems to want to turn toward home. The other day, I was dashing from one errand to another when my car suddenly took the "home" exit. I had to turn around to get back on the highway heading out instead of in. Dear Lord, do you think my car is telling me it's tired and I look tired, too? Maybe I dash about too much when I should be reprogramming myself to spend more time in meditation instead of "motor-zation" and let my wise old auto rest a bit.

Maybe I'm the one who oughta know better.

Don't Fence Me In!

Now I know just how Tom Sawyer felt: It had been a fence-painting week at my house, and I was the paintee. I tried to tell my son how much fun it was and offered to let him have a turn—and share the fun with me—but he wasn't buying. He had read the book and seen the movie.

He made a counteroffer and said he would cut the grass while I painted. Although I recognized the danger of ending up with a fence covered with grass-flecked paint, I agreed.

As he mowed, I sloshed and splashed away, hurrying as fast as I could so I would get the job finished before I ran out of paint. Somehow, it didn't work out that way. Speed did not make the paint go farther—and I ran out of paint before I ran out of fence.

But there were just a few boards left in the corner under the apple tree where it's shadowy so maybe nobody will notice. Or maybe in a few days, when I am able to unbend my fingers from their paintbrush grip, I will get ambitious enough to buy more paint and finish the job.

Maybe if I had been able to save all the paint I dripped on the surrounding bushes and flowers, I would have had enough to finish those last few boards. But then I couldn't have had the exclusive neighborhood rights to polka-dotted landscaping.

Actually, the "paint" I was using was cedar stain, a concoction that is thin and splashy—like I imagine Tom Sawyer's whitewash must have been. That was my excuse for polka-dotting myself as well as the flowers and bushes. And soon the muscles under my cedar-stain polka dots—the muscles that had been reaching high and bending low all afternoon—awakened from their long summer nap. And they did not wake up happily.

While I was painting myself again—this time with liniment—I began to think about how today's society seems to have gotten so good at whitewashing, at covering up, making excuses and pointing the finger to put the blame on "somebody else—not me." And it isn't hard to pass around the paintbrush or talk anyone into taking a turn. All too many people are all too willing to wield the whitewash.

But just then, I looked out the window and noticed that my son had left the lawn mower right where he finished cutting instead of putting it away in the garage. I had to stop linimenting and start lamenting. How many times do I have to tell him that lawn mowers belong on the lawn only while mowing?

Dear Lord, what has happened to the once highly principled conscience? Have our think muscles become too weak and sluggish to notice the whitewashing brigades that are trying today to cover up injustice, inequity, immorality, and irresponsibility? Have we become too brainwashed to even notice or recognize the many little whitewash excuses that are becoming a standard part of everyday life? Help us, Lord. Help me. Help me to do as thorough a job of waking up my conscience as I did of waking up my arm, leg, and back muscles today! And thank you, Lord, for liniment.

Money Is the Root of All Upheaval

My teen-age son finally found a summer job. That's the good news. The wait-a-minute news is that it looks like his making money is gonna cost *us* plenty!

He found one of those wonderful healthy jobs—lots of fresh air, sunshine, exercise, activity, and dirt! After a day like that, when he comes home, he no longer drops his clothes on the floor. Now he can just stand them in the corner!

This means good ol' Mom can pre-soak, resoak, wash, rewash, and wring her hands along with the clothes—but the stains, grease, and paint still won't come out. It's a dirty job, so Mom gets to do it!

Of course, we all know Mom's time is worthless so we won't even discuss all the extra time this extra laundry takes. But we also know that those hopelessly stained and faded clothes will probably have to be replaced before school starts. And we know that a few extra tons of bleach and detergent can get expensive. So by the end of the summer, his laundry is gonna take our budget to the cleaners!

But the wash/rinse cycle is nothing compared to the lunch/supper cycle. Do you know what fresh air does to a growing boy's appetite?

Every day he suggests adding just one more thing to his bulging lunch box to tide him over to suppertime. Pretty soon, fixing his lunch will take about as much time as packing a picnic for a family reunion! And supper! I'm beginning to understand how farm ladies feel when they cook for a bunch of hired hands at harvest time.

Oh well, I know I should rejoice because he's getting all that fresh air and sunshine, and I'm grateful that he has a job, *any* job. After all, I was the one who kept praying in the dark of winter, asking God to help with the job search for the heat of summer. And besides, I've always heard it takes money to make money. Now I know what that means.

Unfortunately, family money is sort of like a summer shower. Even when it comes down fast, it dries up in a hurry.

You get a tax refund, but before you can deposit it, the lawn mower dies. The dentist says the kids have no expensive cavities, but on the way home from his office, the car breaks down. You finally get some money saved for a rainy day, and the roof springs a leak. Or your kid gets a summer job.

Dear Lord, I know that somehow it always works out and the money stretches and the rain makes the flowers grow and climbing the rainbow is fun even when there's a pot of beans at the end instead of a pot of gold! So help me remember that as I teeter-totter on the brink, trying to achieve a well-balanced checkbook, outlook, and life. Thank you, Lord, for my son's summer job. But please make autumn fall quickly—before his tainted income bankrupts us!

Weeds in the Family Garden

There's a weed growing in my garden. In fact, it's growing *all over* my garden. It's relentless. It's indestructible. And I love it.

I guess I should be worried about my obvious lack of proper garden manners, put on my white gloves and yank out that intruder. But I can't. And it's all my mother's fault. You see, my mother had this same weed growing in her garden for years. And she loved it, too. Could it be a problem of heredity?

Thinking back, I recall that my mother had messy closets. And I do, too. My mother's laundry usually came out looking like the "before" instead of the "after." Mine does, too. My mother's homemade cakes were always lopsided. Mine are, too. Yes, it is definitely a heredity problem.

But I don't know how we could help loving this particular weed because it is always breaking into bloom. And its blooms are more sky blue than the sky. Whenever I catch a glimpse of all those baby blues winking up at me, I just can't help but want to smile back. So that's why I don't worry too much about the fact that my garden has gone to weed.

I seem to remember that my mother called her weed "Wandering Jude" because of its traveling lifestyle—and she let it wander at will. One summer she did pull up some of it that had finally "gone too far," but then she didn't have the heart to throw it away, so she planted it in a big fancy flower pot and brought it inside to bask in a sunny window. That year we had a weed wandering around *inside* our house as well as outside!

That was also the year when I was of the age to want to wander about myself, going in all directions at once. My mother let me roam but pulled *me* up short whenever I finally "went too far."

When I look at my weedy garden today, it makes me think of a friend whose son was so gifted and intelligent that he won a fine scholarship to a very prestigious university. They were so proud of him, but at the end of the first year, the boy was restless and unhappy. He gave up the scholarship and began hitchhiking around the country, doing odd jobs here and there, discovering America and trying to discover himself. Naturally his parents were distraught. It seemed as though their fine flower of a son had turned into a weed.

After a few years, though, he found a job he loved and with his creative intellect turned it into a fabulous opportunity. He went back to school at night and graduated with honors. Today he has a high-paying executive position, loves his work, and has a wonderful wife and children—a bloomin' success story in the garden of everyday life!

✤

Dear Lord, I guess most of us have a few relatives (especially teenaged ones) who we sometimes think of as weeds. And we might even be tempted to banish them from our garden. But then we look in the mirror and remember that we, too, have had our wandering-weed times and, through it all, you kept giving us second chances—and third and fourth chances—and still loving us all the while.

So the next time I get discouraged by my family weed patch, I'll just think of what Ralph Waldo Emerson said: "What is a weed? A plant whose virtues have not yet been discovered."

Furrowed Eyebrows

Did you know that cats don't have eyebrows? I never spent much time thinking about that until one night I heard a TV comic making jokes about how silly cats look without eyebrows.

The next time my cat stared soulfully into my face (as he often does), I stared back and discovered it's true—no eyebrows. The poor little thing only has three funny-looking whiskers standing straight up on each side of his forehead. This means he can't knit his brows, have a furrowed brow, or raise an eyebrow in surprise or amazement. He can't even frown!

Of course, he can't smile either. Now is that any way to go through life?

But cats have learned—as we all should—that any difficulty can be overcome. Even without eyebrows, my cat can perfectly convey anger, fear, suspicion, and total disgust—and he can shoot all those looks right across the room at my husband.

Since my husband has eyebrows, he shoots the looks right back and for a few minutes, we have a shootout in the family room corral. It's usually a draw.

My husband returns to reading his paper and our brave kitty cat minces around the edge of the room, far away from the other shooter, leaps into my lap and purrs happily, satisfied with his latest skirmish. He has accomplished his mission without the ability to frown. And when you can purr, who needs to smile?

Dear Lord, my cat could teach a lesson to a lot of people who pass up really great opportunities because they think they have a "lack." They say "I can't" to every situation because they don't have the looks, the brains, the training, the education, the money, or whatever they think is absolutely necessary to accomplish the task.

Actually, Lord, I know one of those people very well. I see her every morning in the mirror while I am brushing my teeth. She is often groaning and mumbling, "I have ten things too many to do today. I'll never get it all done. I know I can't. I know I can't. (She obviously *mis*read the book about the little engine that could.)

Yes, Lord, I'm guilty. I get weak in the knees and weak in the head, worrying instead of working. I know you gave us all different talents and abilities. I know I can't climb the highest mountain, catch a shooting star, or even bake the best banana bread. But I also know you are on my side, Lord, and you will help me through this day and every day.

And when I get discouraged, I can just look at my mellow yellow kitty cat with the funny whiskers sticking out of his forehead. If he can convey joy, fear, disdain, and delight without even being able to frown or smile, then I should be able to achieve anything I set my eyebrows on!

Life Is Just a Bowl of Peaches

Everything's been peachy at my house recently. And it's driving me bananas!

Our freezer's so full of frozen peaches that there's little room for any other frozen assets. Our refrigerator's so full of stewed peaches and peach jam, there's little room for ham and bologna. And our tummies are so full of peach pies, peach cobblers, and peach "surprises" that we are ready to join Peaches Anonymous.

This all started about a month ago. The two little peach trees in our backyard have always been a particular delight to me. They never expected me to give them special food, water, care, or even conversation. They just waited there quietly every year to blossom forth in spring and fruit forth in summer with a small harvest of outrageously delicious peaches. We would eat the peaches fresh from the tree, make some peach pies, and share a few with neighbors.

But last year, a spring frost hit at the height of peach-blooming season, so there was not one peach on either tree. I moaned and groaned all summer about no peaches being the pits. This year, I've been moaning and groaning for a different reason.

Those two little trees seemed determined to make up for last year's fruitlessness. They blossomed forth with so much fruit that their branches sagged to the ground. And then, as the little green peaches turned into rich ripe ones, I was bombarded with a bushel and a peck until I had peaches up to my neck!

At first, I was so pleased, playing Farmer Brown, carrying in my crop every day, peeling and pitting and freezing and baking. But then the harvest began to get ahead of me. No matter how many I gave away or how fast I peeled, those peaches seemed to multiply overnight. I began to realize that too much of a good thing could be too much. I was in the pits again!

Dear Lord, forgive me if I seem ungrateful. I still love those little trees, and I'm thankful to have fruit free for the picking and the pitting. But Lord, this has made me think about how some other peachy things in life can also turn into pitfalls. Chocolate is good for the taste buds, but too much is bad for the poundage. TV can be wonderfully entertaining, but too much numbs sensitivity and dumbs imagination. Material possessions are nice to have, but too many can enslave.

And freedom. Ah, fabulous freedom. We all long for it, wait for it as youngsters, demand it as teenagers. But when we get it, sometimes it's so overwhelming we don't know what to do with it. Thank you, Lord, for giving me freedom to choose the work I will do, the dreams I will dream, the life I will lead. But please give me guidance, too, Lord. Help me to avoid the pits and the pitfalls and use my freedom wisely in this pitted but peachy world of yours.

Out on a Limb of the Family Tree

This summer we lost a close family friend. Our Russian olive tree bit the dust when all its leaves left.

It was close because it was planted at the edge of the patio, right outside our kitchen window. It was a friend because it provided cooling shade for the kitchen and a handy landing pad for the birds in the summer. It was always one of the first signs of springtime, with its fluffy little flowers. And in the fall, its hard, green olive-like berries seemed to be a popular bird snack. It did its bit in the winter, too, when ice or snow turned its graceful branches into a lacy frame for the view from the window in our family room.

And all the time it was being friendly, I was complaining about it. Why? Because every time I stepped on the patio there was a new chore for me to do—thanks to my friendly tree.

As soon as I would sweep up the litter from its springtime blossoms, the breeze would blow down another batch to put my broom back into action. Then the falling olives would need sweeping because they were hard enough to turn an ankle and turn a grin into a grinch. And those straggly limbs!

The friendly tree insisted on reaching over path and fence, forever threatening to snag an unwary visitor with a thorny tickle.

So even in the winter, I would find myself out there trimming limbs and trying to jam their uneven thorniness into garbage cans.

So why did I put up with it all these years? Because I loved it, of course. It was a lot of trouble, but it gave us blossoms and shade and branches for bird friends. It couldn't help the fact that it came equipped with thorns and falling olives. It just did what God made it to do.

In fact, it even grew higher and lasted longer than most trees of its kind. That's why there was a tear in my eye when the buzz saw started chopping it down. And now, every time I look out the window, the patio just doesn't seem right. It's neater but emptier. My broom and I are getting a rest. But I miss my troublesome family friend.

Dear Lord, I did not miss the message that my tree was a lot like a family tree. Children can't help causing a lot of trouble when they are babies. They can't help the fact that they need feeding and burping and changing and rocking. And as they grow, they make so many messes for us to clean up that it's easy to get irritated with them and complain all the time.

But as soon as they go away to school or get married or move into their own apartments, the house just doesn't seem the same without them. It's neater but emptier. And lonelier.

Thank you, Lord, for all the troublesome little sprouts and the growing pains of our family tree. Forgive all the complaining and show all us adults how to do as much giggling as griping, realizing that some day we're gonna miss the mess!

Somewhere Over the Rainbow's Flow

Today my cup doth not overflow. My kitchen sink doth. My waste baskets doth. My ironing board doth. And my mouth doth.

I am not in the mood to wash dishes, empty trash, or heat up the iron. I am in the mood to complain—about why my cup is not more fulleth of fame, fortune, fun, and chocolate.

Oh well, what else is neweth?

This syndrome is a chronic condition that returns when the moon is full, half-full, or on the wane—and it is usually triggered by trivial travails rather than tragedies.

Yesterday I was looking forward to a long-planned outing and lots of conversation with an old friend, but at the last minute a household emergency took the time and we had less than two hours for our get-together. It was not enough.

Today I was expecting a check in the mail. When it arrived, it was for only half what I was expecting. It was not enough.

Recently I have been on a diet, eating only rabbit food for what seems like several centuries, but this morning I stepped on the scale and discovered I had lost only half a pound. It was not enough.

I have always hated that song that asks the question, "Is that all there is?" But I must admit it keeps running through my head today. And why not? There is nothing important enough in today's head to keep a song from romping through!

I've been trying to be positive and concentrate on that story about a glass half-filled with milk. The pessimist saw the glass as half-empty. The optimist saw it as half-full.

I should be seeing my week's nonaccomplishments as half-a-success instead of half-a-failure. But I keep thinking about how much I hate the taste of milk. That means that if the people in that story both hated milk, when the pessimist saw the glass as half-empty, he would have felt good, but the optimist who saw it as half-full would have felt bad. And that would ruin the point of the story.

Whew! In today's mood, I have even managed to runneth down a good story! And I have spent so much time in runneth off and runneth down that too many minutes have runneth out of my clock and now my day's chores will have to be done on the run!

Dear Lord, what am I gonna do with this day? Maybe I could call a friend to come over and help me unfloweth my sink, wastebaskets, ironing board, and mouth. But who could I call? If I call a pessimist, she might depress me even further. And if I call an optimist and she comes in smiling, singing, and dripping her sunshine all over my kitchen floor, I might have to pour a half-glass of milk over her head. Well, Lord, as usual, you see who I called. Yep, it's you, Lord, to the rescue. Remind me again how lucky I am to have such an overabundance in my house. And thank you, Lord, for listening. I needed that.

Best-Laid Plans

I never liked yellow cats. I always thought gray-striped cats or mysterious black cats with yellow eyes or fluffy beige cats with white boots were more interesting.

So, of course, I have a yellow cat.

I didn't plan it that way. He was a neighbor's cat who came to our yard to visit. Then he began coming back every day and staying longer at each visit—until he was spending more time at our house than the one where he was supposed to live. Finally, his owner (who had two other cats and three dogs) said, "Take my cat—please."

Since then, I have had to buy lots of gold jewelry to match all the little golden kitty cat hairs deposited on my dark slacks and sweaters by this little fur person who is always curling up in my lap and purring the message that he likes living at our house.

Other cats might be more regal, stylish, or pedigreed. This one pursues a gentle, comfortable lifestyle. He makes few demands, snuggles down in a spot of sun on the carpet, and often speaks to me in that purry language that sounds like the whir of a wind-up toy.

I didn't want a yellow cat, but I'm glad I have one.

I never liked Japanese cars. I thought others looked more sporty and exciting, and cars made closer to home would be more dependable and easier to get repaired. And besides, anybody who talks to a car as much as I do shouldn't have one that speaks a foreign language.

So, of course, I have a Japanese car.

I didn't plan it that way. When I decided my old beat-up jalopy needed a retirement plan, I went shopping for a bright new American-made car that would give me good gas mileage and a better image. I found some great cars that had everything I was looking for—except the price tag. Then I went shopping for a *used* car with a more friendly price tag.

One day I stopped at a used-car lot, took one look at a shiny red used Japanese car with silver spoke wheels and knew it was "mine." I tried to resist. I tried to find some fault when I took it for a test drive, but everything was perfect. I knew I might as well buy it or it would follow me home.

Since then, we have happily traveled the road together with very few repair bills and very many miles to the gallon.

I never liked the idea of being a housewife—a job that required cooking and cleaning, discipline and diplomacy. I thought I was more suited to be a movie star, astronaut ,or self-made millionaire.

So, of course, I became a housewife. And lived scrappily but happily ever after.

Dear Lord, I guess you knew I needed a little yellow cat to calm me, a little red car to scoot me about, and the title "housewife" to keep my nose to the grindstone and out of international politics. You *do* have a way of changing my best-laid plans. Thank you, Lord, for your better-laid plans. Every day I am reminded of that beautiful meditation, "I got nothing I asked for but everything I hoped for. I am among all people most richly blessed." And I rejoice.

Brown-Bag Banter

B rown-bagging is not my bag. Even when I was a kid, I could not get excited about spending noontime with a little sack that held a soggy sandwich, crumbled cookies, and a bruised banana.

But in recent years, the brown bag has become acceptable or even fashionable. You can even purchase designer lunch bags that don't get saggy or crumble or bruise. Many people have discovered that eating in is faster, less expensive, and lets you count your own calories.

All those benefits make brown-bagging practical and reasonable—so that's probably why I don't like the custom. Practicality and reasonableness have never played prominent parts in my lifestyle. But I *do* get a chuckle every time I see a brown bag because of the time a friend tried to use a brown bag for "medicinal" purposes.

He had been having a problem with hyperventilation, so the doctor said the next time he had trouble breathing, he should put a brown bag over his head for a few minutes. Evidently that's a strange but routine suggestion to help with such a problem.

One day my friend brought doughnuts to the office for breakfast and left the empty bag sitting on his desk. Later in the morning, he felt a breathing attack coming on and grabbed up the doughnut bag and put it over his head. As he sat at his desk with a bag on his head and powdered sugar sifting over his shoulders, the boss brought in an important client to meet his "star" employee. The scene made a big impression on boss and client—but it was not a good career move.

Every time I remember that story, I think about how paper bags are a lot like people. You can't judge what's inside by the way they look on the outside. Two bags can look pretty much alike, but inside one you might find powdered doughnuts and inside the other, expensive imported caviar. You have to look inside to tell the difference. And even then, you have to judge for yourself which is better—the doughnuts or the caviar.

It's so easy to take people at face value—to never try to see inside to learn what makes them tick or makes them hurt.

It's so easy to let others keep a bag over their head if you are hiding under your own bag. And that's not a pretty sight.

Dear Lord, I am one of the bag people. I sometimes hide behind my own false face, keeping others away, never letting them come close enough to see my hurts and hopes. And I let my friends get away with the same trick—instead of trying to look behind their "face value." Help me to change that, Lord. Help me to start seeing my friends as old bags. No, no, that's not quite right, is it, Lord? Help me to get to know my baggy friends better—and allow them to know me better, too.

But Lord, if you see me sitting in a corner with a bag over my head, don't worry. I'm probably not hiding or having trouble breathing. I'm probably just trying to get that last bite of powdered sugar from the morning doughnuts.

Stressed and Undressed Furniture

The naked eye, the naked truth, the naked city. Yes, I've heard of all those—but naked furniture?

The other day, I stopped at a red light alongside a truck with a huge sign on its side that advertised "Naked Furniture."

After a while I realized it must mean unpainted furniture, but for a few minutes I was considering a truckload of tables with bare legs, sofas with bare arms, and chairs with bare backs!

Then I began to think about all the naked furniture in our house. There's the yellow bookcase that has a lot of naked places where the paint has been nicked off by years of book satchels being tossed on it, keys being dropped on it, and toy cars being raced into it.

The bedroom furniture has a few naked nicks and notches that I tried to fix with the help of a brown crayon. The magazine article I read said that a brown crayon would work every time—but I guess nothing works every time. So I decided the only answer was "subdued" lighting and put forty-watt bulbs in that room.

But there is actually only one piece of furniture in the house that ever got to the point where it needed a bathrobe to cover its naked wood—the old chest in the family room. When we first got married, I dragged that chest out of somebody's basement and painted it pink. That seemed like a good idea at the time.

After a few years, "being in the pink" didn't seem so cute any more, and the poor old chest got dragged to *our* basement. But one day I felt real ambitious and decided something could be done with it. Off to the hardware store I trotted for some paint stripper, and soon I was elbow-deep in oozing pink paint and gooey stripper dripping all over everywhere.

Since I had never done that kind of job before—and never will again—I expected the naked wood to have a rich, warm shine with honeyed golden undertones like the beautiful old furniture I see in antique stores. Wrong! It just looked like a boring board.

On a return trip to the hardware store, I was told it was up to me to add a finish and rub and buff and work to bring out the grain and reveal the richness that was in the wood just waiting to shine forth.

Now when I look at that burnished and beautiful chest, I some-times think of how much we are all like "naked" furniture. We might not like to see what's under our paint or veneer. We might be shocked at how bare of beauty it is. If we're honest enough to look at the nicks and notches, we might just cover them up. We might not be willing to do all the rubbing and buffing needed to let our true beauty shine forth.

Dear Lord, you and I know it's time for a fix-it-yourself project. It's a project that will take a lot of sweat, tears, and exasperation, a project that will never be really finished—and the object of the project is *me*. My family and friends are sometimes *too* willing to point out my nicks and notches but Lord, you and I know that I'm the one who will have to add the finishing touches to bring out the richness you gave me. Thank you, Lord, for all the possibilities—but don't be surprised if I come crying to you for help when the paint starts oozing and the stripping starts dripping.

Earmuffs

Every morning, our meowser insists on going out to make his neighborhood rounds no matter how cold the weather. And when he returns, even if there's snow on his toes, it seems his yellow fur coat has kept him all snug and warm—except for his perky stand-up ears. They're cold enough to be ear-sickles.

So I let him curl up in the chair with me and I rub his ears until they get all warmed up. Then he purrs his thanks and goes on his way—never knowing that a pair of teeny, tiny earmuffs could make his life much more comfortable.

I remember the poem about the three little kittens who lost their mittens, but I never heard one about cat earmuffs. Now that they make coats and hats and even sunglasses for cats and dogs, I could probably find some muffs if I shopped long enough. But I wonder why God didn't give cats total protection instead of leaving that one small vulnerable spot.

On the other hand, why should cats be invincible when people aren't? It seems that even the strongest, bravest, truest, most heroic human usually has some small area of vulnerability, a soft spot that needs protection.

Most humans have some sore spots—disappointments, dreams dashed, wishes unfulfilled, loneliness, fear, anger. But instead of dwelling on them, perhaps we should be grateful for those little spots of vulnerability. My kitty cat's vulnerable ears give him the opportunity to get sympathy, ear rubs, and lots of attention. In the same way, our vulnerabilities often give us the need—and the opportunity—to reach out to others.

When we admit our humanness and reach out to *ask* for help, we open a door to admit friendship and love. When we reach out to *offer* help, we give others the same opportunity. Either kind of reaching can add a new dimension and a new warmth to our sometimes cold everyday life.

Dear Lord, You know I never have trouble reaching out to ask *you* for help, but sometimes it's harder to ask for a human helping hand. Forgive my pride and my selfishness. Help me to reach out and touch someone—not by telephone but in person. And Lord, forgive me if I don't try *too* hard to find those cat earmuffs. My cat probably wouldn't wear them anyway and besides, I enjoy curling up in my chair for furry-purry sessions with those frosty little ears.

Sink or Swim

When I go swimming, it is not a pretty sight. Some little children take one look at me, shriek, and head for the other end of the pool. Other children follow me around, staring. And I don't blame them. Since I hate to get water in my nose, I wear a strange black nose clip that makes me look like a walrus.

It all started when I took my first swimming lesson. We didn't live near water when I was a child, so I never learned. And when I was a teenager, I was nonliberated enough to think that all a girl was supposed to do at a pool was sit around in a new bathing suit, trying to hold her tummy in and keep her hair—and suit—dry. Finally, as a young adult, I decided to take the plunge and enrolled in a swim class.

At "graduation" time, when all the other students were valiantly paddling across the pool, I had just gotten brave enough to float on my back—but not my front. Determined, I re-enrolled and took the same class a second time.

By now the instructor had noticed I did not like to get water in my nose and presented me with a wonderful gift—the nose clip. This was not a dainty, skin-colored clip like they sell in sporting goods stores. It was just the kind I needed—heavy-duty. It had two thick black rubber pads that fit at each side of the nose that were joined by an ominous-looking silvery wire coil that went under the nose and acted like a spring to keep your nostrils glued shut.

It looked like it might have been the nose decoration of an African tribal dancer at an ancient voodoo ceremony. And maybe that's what it was, because when I wore that clip, it worked magic.

It looked so forbidding that the water parted like the Red Sea and never a drop dared think of entering my nose. Soon I was swimming across the pool like the rest of the class. I was so inspired that I continued into the intermediate class and even beyond. Eventually, I could even jump off the side of the pool and swim laps. It was a miracle!

In all the years since, I have treasured my nose clip the way others treasure Grandma's silver service. I never leave home for the pool without it. And when I get into the pool with it, the kids are staring, the adults are snickering, and the lifeguard is watching me suspiciously.

Dear Lord, forgive me for being so dependent on that silly nose clip. I could probably swim just as well without it, but I don't want to try it. I guess there are a lot of other things that I cling to, foolishly thinking I couldn't survive without them. I know I could, Lord, I just don't want to try. I guess I'm lazy, Lord. It's so comfortable to have something familiar to hang on to and depend on. Help me, Lord, to be less dependent on things and more dependent on you. But please let me keep that nose clip, Lord—it's so much fun to be the only walrus in the pool!

Thanks for the Memories

I love to laugh. I love to go to funny movies and hear funny jokes and look at funny pictures. Maybe that's why I love my ancestors. The pictures of them in my family album are the funniest pictures I've ever seen!

There's Uncle Pink and Uncle Ransom and Uncle Grover Cleveland McCarver. There's Aunt Oskie in her ostrich-feather hat, Grandma in the coat with the big bearskin collar, and solemn, bug-eyed Great-Grandma, who looks like someone just told her the end of the world would be Thursday and she was the one chosen to fry enough chicken to feed everybody who showed up.

I got out the old album the other day when I read an article by a clinical psychologist who said body language in old photos could tell you a lot about your family.

According to the learned doctor, there are a lot of hidden messages in those old faded faces. You're supposed to look and see who's standing next to whom, who's smiling at whom, who looks mad, who looks sad, and who's hiding behind a bush.

The psychologist thinks if you never see a husband and wife pictured together, maybe that's because they're trying to pretend they don't know each other. Personally I think it's just because somebody has to take the picture and they don't want to trust that expensive camera to one of the kids. But maybe that's why he's a famous psychologist and I'm hiding behind a bush.

Whatever those old photos say to you, looking at them is sure a fun way to spend a rainy afternoon. I love to look at Daddy standing on the boardwalk at Atlantic City. He's wearing a three-piece suit and a Panama hat while everybody in the background is in bathing suits! There's my young and beautiful mother posing coyly under a Chinese paper parasol, and my adorable nephew, at age five, sitting on a mule and grinning through a face full of dirt. And in every single shot since her baby picture, my sister has the same sweet smile that she always wore throughout her life. The fashions in the photos changed but not her smile.

They say photographs are one of the first things people try to save when there's a fire in the house. And no wonder. They are irreplaceable reminders of family history, special ceremonies, and the people, places, and milestones of life. That's why looking at them can open a window to yesterday that gives us glimpses of values and hopes and dreams—a solid foundation on which to build the future. And a lot of laughs.

Dear Lord, it's easy to make fun of the way things used to be instead of appreciating the lessons that can be learned there. It's easy to blame the mistakes we make today on the way we were treated or taught or spoiled or neglected in the past. Help me, Lord, to learn from—and forgive—the past. Help me to sort through and throw out the trash but save the treasure. And thank you, Lord, for Uncle Pink and Aunt Oskie, for Great-Grandma's frown, and my sister's sweet smile. Thank you for yesterday and today.

Of Bags and Baggage

He who steals my purse steals trash." But it's trash I can't live without!

It doesn't make sense, I know, but a woman has this built-in unquenchable desire to have some kind of bag hanging from her arm. I bet if you could find an actual photograph of Eve, she would be clutching a leaf purse with a grapevine handle. She may not have had any clothes, but you can bet she had a purse!

Wherever you go—a grocery, ball game, dance, movie, fire sale, or hayride—you'll see all the women there clutching purses. If you see one without a purse, she is probably wringing her hands because she doesn't know what to do with them when they are purse-less.

Just the other day I saw a photograph of Queen Elizabeth at some royal function. She was wearing a jeweled evening gown and a diamond tiara, but hanging from a dangling chain over her white-gloved arm was this purse big enough to hold the Magna Carta. It didn't go with the outfit, but I'm sure it made her feel secure.

The next day I saw a lady in a leather lumberjack-type jacket, heavy slacks, and boondocker shoes, but dangling from her leather-gloved hand was a dainty ladylike purse. Again, it didn't go with the outfit but she looked very secure. Who can explain it, who can tell me why? Fools give you reasons, wise men never try.

A woman's purse is her survival kit, security blanket, and badge of authority all rolled into one. So how do men manage without one?

I think it's because whenever they need anything, they turn to a woman and say, "Look in your purse and see if you have some fishing twine. How about a screwdriver? Is there a bandage in there? Do you have the phone number of the auto repair shop, the hardware store, and the Burger Barn?" I suspect they don't carry purses because they don't have to!

Dear Lord, I've noticed that, with or without a purse, most of us carry around some excess baggage—and it's the kind of baggage we should leave in the will-call and then lose the claim ticket. I seem to recall that the Latin word for baggage is *impedimenta,* and that's just what baggage does—it impedes our progress. When a woman's purse gets so full it weighs as much as a barbell, she can't just snatch it up and run. She has to drag it along behind her. And the same thing happens when we get so full of fear or guilt or doubt or worry. We are no longer free. Everywhere we go, we have to drag along all that baggage.

Well, Lord, I am starting right now to clean out my purse— but I know it won't be as easy to clean out all that other stuff. Help me, Lord, to get rid of fears from the past and stop laying claim to them. Help me to give up guilt and trust in your forgiveness. Help me to pitch out doubt and worry. And Lord, please help me get this gumdrop loose that is stuck to the lining of my purse!

Don't Tell Alexander Graham Bell

No one could ever accuse my husband of being a phony. He spends as little time as possible on the telephone and thinks three or four sentences should be adequate for anyone to get any message across to anyone else. And then it's time to hang up.

Evidently he managed to program himself to use the phone for business purposes, but he could never understand anyone voluntarily choosing to use it for social chitchat. Maybe that's why he finds it totally beyond his realm of possibility to take telephone messages for me.

For example, we were sitting quietly watching the news on TV one evening when a newsman named John appeared on the screen. This seemed to trigger a distant spot in my husband's memory bank. He said, "That reminds me. Someone named Joan called you last week." I said, "Joan? Joan who?"

He thought for a minute and then responded, "Maybe it wasn't Joan. It might have been Jean or June or Jan. Anyway, she wanted you to call her back right away."

Right away? I could lose a lot of friends like that!

Another time, the message came only a day late—but it was a bit garbled. My husband suddenly said, "Oh, by the way, some missionary called you yesterday."

Missionary? What kind of missionary and why was he calling? My husband couldn't remember any further details or whether there had been a message. I spent a couple days wondering who I knew who might have an urgent message for me from some far-flung mission outpost. Then I received a call from a local store.

They said they had called me earlier to tell me the "Franciscan Ware" dishes I ordered had come in—and were wondering why I hadn't come in to pick them up. Missionary indeed!

Dear Lord, fortunately the communication problem at my house is limited to telephone calls, but there seems to be a more serious communication gap in society at large. Teachers, parents, children, politicians, and school bus drivers all complain that nobody listens to them. Help us, Lord. Remind us to pay more attention to what others are trying to tell us.

I know I have sometimes been guilty, Lord, of half-listening, interrupting in the middle of a sentence, daydreaming, or thinking of what I want to say next instead of really concentrating on what the other person is saying—and trying to understand *her* side of the story before I begin to present *mine*.

Help me, Lord, to give my undivided attention and *listen* to others—and to you. And, Lord, could you please appear to my husband in a vision and tell him to start *writing down* my phone messages?

New and Improved?

My house is full of sows' ears. My trash is stuffed with silk purses. And I bet you have the same problem.

It has always been the American way to want to improve everything—to try to make silk purses out of sows' ears.

Politicians are always begging for votes by promising to take the sow by the ear and give us a "change" in government. Parents are always struggling to give their children a "better" life than they've had. And half the products in any store have the same magic words on their labels—"new and improved."

But recently I've noticed something scary. We seem to have stopped trying to improve the product and are only interested in improving the *package*. I go to the store and buy the same old something I've been buying for years—but now it's packaged in six layers of plastic, attached to a flower-decorated piece of cardboard, and costs twice as much as before. It takes a pair of scissors, a kitchen knife, and two broken fingernails to get it open, and then I throw the silk-purse packaging in the trash and put the same old sow's ear on my shelf.

When we get the same old product but are told it's new and improved because of its packaging, we are given the message that only the packaging is important. It's what's outside that counts—not what's inside.

The same is true of TV programming. If the show is packaged with a beautiful star, fancy settings, and a laugh track, who complains about the fact that some of the characters are totally immoral, the situations make fun of traditional values, and the lines are just a little dirty?

And that, of course, brings us to today's people. If they're "packaged" correctly—in expensive clothes, with important friends, a fancy car, and a "good" address—do we care if they have interior spirituality, morals, or values? If they look young and "with it," do we think that's more important than the wisdom of maturity? If they have a stylish hairdo on the outside of the head, do we let that influence us more than what's going on inside the head?

Dear Lord, have you noticed how easy it is for me to criticize all those *other* people for their silk-purseness when I am sometimes guilty of the same kind of packaging? I may drag around the house in an old bathrobe until it's time to leave for a luncheon, and then I try to package myself in the proper clothes, hairdo, and makeup. I may still look as bad as I did in the bathrobe, but I *do* waste time trying.

Forgive me, Lord, for being concerned about the outside of myself *and* others. Help me to be discerning and look beyond the packaging—both of people *and* of ideas. And thank you, Lord, for all the "surprise packages" you've sent me. I've sometimes hated the wrappings—until I got inside and found the blessings!

Feathering the Nest With Dad

Today's dads could learn a thing or two from the male emperor penguin. He's a real bird of a father!

It seems that all the mother penguin does is lay one single egg and her job is finished. Then she flies away from home, abandoning the nest—except she hasn't even bothered to do any home building so there *is* no nest. She just takes off and leaves the old man standing out in the cold.

The father emperor penguin hatches the offspring by standing upright and holding the egg *on top of his feet* for two months!

Do you realize what that means? No fly-by-nights out with the boys, no bowling or golf or baseball—and no food! Once Mom decides she deserves a break today and leaves, she doesn't even fly by with a bag of burgers until after the chick is hatched. Now there is a liberated mother. *And* a dedicated father.

Meanwhile, back in the human kingdom, the feat of fathering is going through some dramatic changes. Role models are shifting, and more fathers are helping with housework and cooking and child-care (at least that's what I read in the papers, although I don't see a lot of it in my immediate neighborhood)!

But as mothers are finally getting a better image and being recognized and respected for their qualities and equality, the image of fathers may be suffering. There was a time when a father was depicted and visualized as a tower of strength, the bread-winner, the provider, the strong arm to lean on, the protector, the honorable man.

Only occasionally would there be an exception—like the cartoon of Dagwood Bumstead. He was the well-meaning but absent-minded goof-off, the forgetful sleepyhead. And people laughed because he was not really typical—not really the image most people had of a father.

Unfortunately, today it seems fathers are *usually* depicted as the bumbler—in commercials, movies, and TV programs. Today, fathers just "don't get no respect."

Maybe in the past we expected too much of dads, expecting them to be always in charge, the leader, the one responsible for guidance and discipline, and the very bread of life. Or maybe we asked too little, leaving them on the sidelines when it came to nurturing.

Maybe we should all take a more realistic look at the role of fatherhood and the role we *all* play in either ridiculing it or honoring it. Maybe we've been leaving fathers out in the cold like that poor emperor penguin!

✛

Dear Lord, have I spent so much time feeling sorry for myself that I didn't have enough left over to notice the problems of others—like the problems of fathers? Forgive me, Lord. Help me to be less ready to ridicule and more eager to honor. Remind me that we all have different roles to play, but each is as important as the other—and as difficult.

Thank you, Lord, for all the fathers who have come into my life at different times and made it more comfortable, more interesting, and more fun—my own father, grandfather, and husband plus fathers who have been neighbors, business acquaintances, or good friends. Help them all, Lord. And help the rest of us to be more concerned with their feelings and "give them more respect!"

Throwing a
Temperature Tantrum

S ome people blow hot and cold. I know. I'm one of them.
Like Goldilocks tasting the porridge, I test the temperature
and usually find it "too hot" or "too cold." I never seem to feel "just
right." Instead, I'm either burning up or freezing. My husband says
my thermostat must be broken.

His temperature is always the same. Some like it hot. He likes
it cold. But even more than cold, he likes "fresh air." All year he's
opening windows to "air out the house"—summer, winter, rain,
snow, or whatever. As a result, our house is sometimes a sauna
and often a refrigerator. Since my broken thermostat can't adjust
to that, I've become a quick-change artist.

In the summer, with windows open, I've got on shorts and a
blouse, dashing about doing chores. Then, just when I've worked
up a lather, my husband starts closing windows. On comes the air
conditioner, and gusts of frigid air pour onto my sweltering brow.
It's time to change into slacks and a sweater.

But when house chores are finished, there's yard work to do,
and that means changing back to the shorts, since you can't garden
while dressed like Nanook of the North. When I've conquered the
great outdoors, it's time to head for the grocery—but the grocery
is air-conditioned so it's time to change again.

When I put on the high-necked, long-sleeved grocery store clothes, they're too hot to be comfortable "in transit." The obvious solution is the automobile's air conditioning, but my husband warns me that my old car's old air conditioner is bad for the old car's old motor. He suggests that instead of using it, I should open all the car windows because I will *enjoy* all that nice, fresh air.

You can see that I am in danger of having a temperature tantrum at all times!

Dear Lord, at least I get a lot of exercise running back and forth to the closet. Maybe I should be grateful for that. And besides, I've noticed that I'm not the only quick-change artist who blows hot and cold. There are politicians who constantly change campaign promises, corporate executives who suddenly change the rules of the game and the office, and kids who can be angels one minute and not the next. Help us all, Lord, and forgive our quick changes. As we wander and wonder, changing, learning, seeking guidance, show us the way. Remind us to pray more so that, some day, we will stop blowing hot and cold and learn how to live "just right."

Double-Time, Double Takes, and Double Jeopardy

My cat is leading a double life. At home, he meekly sits by the fireside, napping and purring, a picture of contentment and tranquility. Sometimes he curls up in my lap, keeping one eye half-open, just in case an enemy (like my husband) should appear. Other times, he quietly munches the cat yummies in his little bowl in a kitchen corner or sits staring out the window, keeping his feline feelings to himself.

But when he goes *out*, that's a different story. He steps softly through the patio door and turns into Adventure Cat. He scampers across the lawn, sharpens his claws on the big oak, then lurks in the bushes, crouched like a lion, pretending to guard our backyard. He climbs our trees and has been known to leap our tall fence in a single bound.

No wonder we're such good friends. He reminds me a little of myself and all of today's "working" women who lead a double life.

We, too, sometimes sit meekly by the fireside, napping and purring, with one eye open to what's going on around. We, too, quietly munch our diet meals of celery, carrot sticks, and chocolate bars in a kitchen corner (so no one will notice there's more chocolate than carrots)! We, too, give the appearance of contentment and tranquility. But when we go *out*—that's a different story.

A "working" woman who has a career, or at least a "paid position," is expected to step softly through her front door and become Executive Woman! She must be alert, efficient, well-informed, and well-dressed, prepared to make decisions instantly and logically (not sentimentally) and be able to leap every crisis in a single bound.

A "working" woman who does not have a career is expected to behave in exactly the same way when she steps through her front door to assume such "unpaid positions" as chairperson of a committee, coordinator of school or church activities, club president, or general in charge of whatever happens in general.

And in addition to keeping the home fires burning and setting the world on fire, all "working" women have those endless little chores and errands to run—trips to the cleaners, gas station, drugstore, hardware store, grocery store. Oh yes, always and forever, trips to the grocery store.

Somehow this double life doesn't seem as much fun as climbing trees or flying over fences, but at least there's never a dull moment—because we never know when an emergency will strike and Executive Woman must charge forth to the rescue!

Dear Lord, I guess I should stop spending so much time complaining about this double life and realize that's the way the world is today. This is my culture, my era, the way my world operates. Help me, Lord, to understand that but not just accept it as is. Help me to keep trying to improve it and make it better for myself and for my family. Remind me, Lord, of that Chinese proverb, "A wise person learns to adapt to circumstances as water shapes itself to the vessel that contains it." Teach me, Lord, to adapt but not settle. Help me to keep trying to improve this vessel—and to appreciate and enjoy the double blessings in this double life.

Anyone for Tea?

Ahhhfternoon teatime...fine china, silver, crumpets, and cake...one lump or two? How veddy sophisticated and elegant.

Although sophistication is not exactly my cup of tea, I got all excited when I saw a newspaper ad announcing that high tea was now being served every afternoon at one of our fanciest downtown hotels. My friend Mary's birthday was approaching, and this seemed like a jolly good way to celebrate.

So Mary and I got all gussied up and headed downtown. As we approached the front of the hotel, I slowed to look for a parking spot but, before I had time to think about it, a hotel attendant was approaching, offering to park the car for me. Since I was feeling rather regal, as visions of sugarplums and teacups danced in my head, I handed him my car keys—with pinkie finger extended—and toddled off to tea.

It was even nicer than we had expected—specially blended tea, tiny finger sandwiches, lovely little cakes, and chocolate-dipped strawberries. And they even brought Mary a yellow rose for her birthday while the person tickling the ivories on the baby grand piano played an appropriately demure "Happy Birthday to You."

We sipped and chewed as slowly as possible, stretching out the treat as long as we could, but finally it was time to return to the real world. We must have emerged from the hotel at checkout/check-in time because we stepped into a whirl of very fancy activity—a white-gloved doorman welcoming guests who had just arrived in a looong stretch limo, a swanky black import car waiting for its driver, cabs darting in and out, picking up or letting out people who were dressed as if they went to high tea every day.

Suddenly it dawned on me that at any moment this world of affluence was going to be jarred by an attendant driving my old rust bucket—the ancient one that's now trimmed with a lacy fringe of rust along the underside and a designer decoration of jagged rust-outs on each front fender.

The vision of Mary and me as members of the peerage turned to thoughts of steerage as we scurried to get in the car as fast as possible and remove our rustiness before we besmirched the beautiful-people picture.

Oh well, it was fun while it lasted. And besides, it was nice to get home, kick off the high heels, and snuggle back into my little nest. It's good to fly high occasionally, but there's no place like home—even if it has a mortgage and rust spots.

Dear Lord, I know that poor is not necessarily better than rich. I once read a quote that went something like this: "Pharmacists have many kinds of poisons, but they do not get poisoned themselves because they keep the poisons in their shops, not in their bodies. In the same way, you may possess riches without being poisoned by them—*if* you keep them in your house or purse but not in your heart."

So I know, Lord, that wealthy is as wealthy does—just like the rest of us. Thank you, Lord, for my snug little nest and the delicious high tea. But Lord, help me to remember that wealth, like beauty, is only skin deep and finger sandwiches are just plain old ham-on-white—without the upper crust.

The Treasured Dowry

The strangest thing happened today. Out of nowhere, I began thinking about my former life—those single, carefree days when I moved into my first apartment.

Luckily it was furnished, since all I had to bring to it were some clothes, an old typewriter, one set of new sheets, and one pillow. On my first day off from work, I hurried to a small neighborhood store to buy some luxurious apartment additions—cheap pots, pans, and dishes.

For some strange reason, the only plates in that store had scalloped edges, and there were holes in the scallops so you could run ribbon through them. Obviously, these plates were meant for a wall, not a table, but I was desperate so I bought two of them. Today most stores have pretty paper plates and even nicer decorated plastic ones. But not that day.

I couldn't wait to have my first company dinner, so I invited the girl who lived across the hall to join me that very night. We had just met, so she didn't know any better and accepted the invitation.

Since I didn't know how to cook *anything*, spaghetti seemed the easiest thing to try. It may have been easy to cook, but we soon discovered that spaghetti was not easy to eat when you had plates with holes on the edges. Instead of ribbon running through them, spaghetti and sauce kept running through. It was an almost inedible, incredibly giggly meal, and I'll never forget it.

Soon I found another store and other plates, then added another luxurious kitchen addition—a hand-held toaster. On one of my bargain-seeking expeditions, I found this strange little wire grill in which you encased one piece of bread. You were supposed to hold the grill over an open gas flame until the bread scorched and then turn it over to scorch the other side.

I think I may have been one of the few persons in history to ever own such an item. It was a wonderful conversation piece, though, and also provided me with some very unusual breakfasts.

As I continued trying to upgrade my standard of living to the level of minimum, I added a well-used easy chair (so well-used, it was *over* easy), an old trunk I pretended was a coffee table, and a bookcase that was being trashed by its former owner. By the time I met Prince Charming, I had a dowry full of such "finds."

We continued using some of my dowry items for years, but my husband never did warm up to that open-flame toaster. My mother took pity on him and gave us an electric toaster, which served us well for years until I was lured by a shiny new toaster on sale and decided to upgrade our standard of living again.

It was a mistake. The new one is already rejecting rye and tossing wheat and white across the table. They just don't make things like they used to—in my former life.

Dear Lord, shiny and new is nice but not always better. I've noticed that toasters are not the only things that don't last as long any more. Christmas toys were once so durable they could be handed down to the next generation. Now they may not last until New Year's Day! Help us, Lord, to hold tight to our old tried and true morals and values in these changing times. And Lord, I know that *you* still make things like you used to—babies with little pink toes, sunsets, rainbows, and flowers that bloom in the spring, tra la. Thank you, Lord, thank you.

A Once-Upon-a-Time Story With a Happy Ending

I just heard a wonderful story that happened many years ago. Today it would *not* be politically correct and would seem unseemly to many, but I think it's inspiring!

I don't know what year it was, but it was a time when few young people went to college and many never even graduated from high school. There was this bright, hard-working teenager who had to drop out of school to go to work when he finished eighth grade. He was very ambitious, though, and his goal was to work for the biggest company in town. There was only one problem—you had to have a high school education before you could apply for a job there.

To most, this would have seemed like an insurmountable obstacle, but he had a plan. His parents had a good friend who was a high school teacher, and he went to her and told her about his dream and his plan. She must have recognized his potential because she agreed to help.

She met him at the front door of her school and walked with him through the building. Then she gave him a signed note stating that he had "gone through" that high school.

With that piece of paper as his credential, he got the job. Although he was technically unqualified, he dedicated himself to the work, soon became a valued employee, and worked for the company for many years. When he finally left, it was to found his own company and become a very successful businessman and respected community leader.

In today's world of rules and regulations, that story would probably raise a lot of eyebrows and maybe some ethical questions. But the world was different then and times were hard. That teacher's note changed a young man's life—and perhaps changed many other lives that his work touched in later years—just as the Good Samaritan changed the life of a man in need.

Dear Lord, thank you for the many dedicated teachers, both in the past and present. I will never forget and be forever grateful to the wonderful teachers who influenced my life from first grade to today. There have also been many teachers who became personal friends and good role models through the years. Thank you for the privilege of knowing them, Lord. And thank you, Lord, for being the best teacher of all. I don't always like your rules, but I know you know what you're doing—and I know I don't. Please continue to teach me, Lord, as I "go through" the school of life.

The Lopsidedness of Life

I had a close call in the kitchen today. I almost broke a treasured family tradition—by baking a nonlopsided cake.

Sometime in the distant past, my son decided his favorite dessert in the world was my yellow cake with chocolate-almond icing. Since then, he's always requested that cake for every birthday and special occasion. The invited guests at these occasions could not always understand his enthusiasm for this rather everyday dessert—but to him it was always special.

And it has become a family tradition that every time I have made this no-frills cake, the finished product has turned out lopsided. Either the cake cooked crooked or the cook crooked her finger wrong or whatever—but the top layer would always slide off the bottom layer while I frantically tried to hold back gravity with a spatula, praying for the frosting to harden fast enough to keep the top glued on. Today, for no apparent reason, things were different.

When I finished icing the cake, I suddenly realized something was very wrong. It looked just like other people's cakes. It looked almost like a bakery cake. It was *not* lopsided.

I knew my son would be disappointed, but it was too late to do anything about it. In despair, I started washing up the pots and pans, knowing I had failed the family tradition.

But then, out of the corner of my eye, I sensed movement. Quickly, I checked the cake and, sure enough, the top layer was very slowly sliding sideways. With a great sense of satisfaction—and years of practice—I propped up one side of the cake plate so the top layer would have to stop in mid-slide. Soon the icing hardened and held, and I had a perfect lopsided cake ready for my son to celebrate a traditional birthday!

Dear Lord, sometimes we expect families to be sooo perfect, but sometimes lopsided is more fun—and certainly more realistic! In fact, the lopsided members of my family are the ones we remember the most. We still chuckle about Aunt Linnie, who used to save string and bury silver dollars in her backyard in case paper money became worthless. She was stingy with some things but often very generous to us. Nosy Aunt Ellen could ask twenty-five questions in twenty-four minutes, but at least she was interested in us. And Uncle Grover smoked so many cigars he could sit outside all summer and no mosquito would dare bite him for fear of nicotine poisoning. But he was so kind and gentle, he was my favorite uncle. Thank you, Lord, for all our lopsided relatives. If I ever get impatient with some of the irritating habits of our kith and kin, help me to remember that even the families in Norman Rockwell's paintings had freckles and lopsided smiles—and that's what made them so interesting. Remind me that sometimes lopsidedness is the "icing on the cake!"

A Twist in Time

It's a good thing I didn't get murdered in my sleep last Tuesday night. If I had, the detectives would have been sure to pin it on the wrong person.

As a longtime fan of mystery stories, I know how the questioning goes in a murder case. "Where were you between midnight and 5 a.m.? What was your relationship with the deceased? And why is there a button missing from your raincoat?"

As clues are gathered, speculation begins. Did the butler do it? Or was it the butcher, baker, candlestick maker, or Great-Aunt Sue?

Sometimes the clue that unmasks the guilty turns out to be something as outlandish as a paper clip in an ashtray or an ash on a paper tray. And the minute Chief Inspector Gumshoe spots this clue, the case is solved.

That's why I'm so glad I didn't get murdered Tuesday night. You see, on Wednesday morning, when I made the bed, I found this little twist-tie next to one of the pillows—the kind of tie you usually find on the end of a plastic wrapper that's on the end of a loaf of bread. But not on the end of a bed!

I have no idea what twist of fate put that twist-tie in our bedroom. But since that's just the kind of clue they always get excited about, the inspector probably would have pounced on it and pointed to a perpetrator who was impeccably innocent. As Gumshoe wrapped up the case, he would have said something like, "Aha! A twist-tie from a bread wrapper! Obviously the murderer is—the baker from the bread store where Great-Aunt Sue bought the sourdough roll she dropped in the collection basket at church last Sunday!"

Well, I'm grateful I found that twist-tie before Inspector Gumshoe did. Now that I think about it, the guilty one who left that twist-tie by my pillow was probably the cat! And it could have been worse—the "murderer" *could* have left a dead mouse!

Dear Lord, I confess. False clues have sometimes led me to punish the innocent, excuse the guilty, and point a finger of blame in the wrong direction. I have punished someone for the "crime" of hurting my feelings or my pride when the accused actually meant no harm or insult and should have been treated as innocent until proven guilty. And all too often, the ones who got punished were my nearest and dearest—family and friends. Forgive me, Lord, for my pointing finger. The next time I am tempted to accuse someone, remind me to first ask myself, "Should you be accusing someone 'else' or could *you* be the guilty one? Are *you* the one who done it?"

Mourning in the Morning

One day last week, as I was dashing off to an early appointment, I saw a lady coming out her front door to get the morning newspaper. She was wearing fuzzy house shoes, a pink-flowered robe, a bright red coat thrown around her shoulders, and a fur hat.

That really made my day. All this time I thought I was the only one who dressed like that in the morning.

On days when I have business to conduct, I manage to get up and get dressed properly before leaving the house. But if it's a slow morning and my motor is not turning over yet, I am apt to appear in a strange assortment of clothing as I stumble outside to put the mail in the box or the trash in the can before pickup time.

I don't even think about what I'm wearing until I get back in the house and catch sight of myself in a mirror. One cool spring morning, I saw myself wearing a nightgown, raincoat, rain hat, socks, and house shoes. One cold winter morning, I had on a short hooded jacket over a long robe and snow boots.

Maybe such sights will keep me humble. At least they will help my neighbors open their eyes a little wider in the morning and start the day thinking, "There, but for the grace of God, go I."

But seeing that lady in the fur hat made me realize that I am not the only one who has strange morning habits. Actually, I guess there are a lot of people like me who sometimes think we are the only one—the only one who has a house coming apart at the seams, the only one who hasn't found fame and fortune, the only one who has a sore big toe, the only one who ever does something weird or stupid.

Well, now when I start thinking I am an "only," I will remember that whatever my problem—whether it's a silly little aggravation or a terrible trouble—there are plenty of others who share the same worry. I may not know who they are or where they live, but they are there. And they might live right in my own neighborhood.

Knowing others have problems does not diminish mine, but it is somehow reassuring to know that there are others who are also searching and stumbling—and surviving. I am not alone.

Dear Lord, it's easy to think that I am unique—that I am the only one who is lazy or messy or disorganized or tired. It's easy to think that I am the only nonachiever or the only one who can't make gelatin jell. Thank you, Lord, for showing me that I am never the only one. And, Lord, I am going to be more careful in the future when I step out the door in the morning. But Lord, are you *sure* I'm not the only one who can't make those gelatin molds mold?

The Frill of It All

When I was at that dangerous teen age, my mother thought if one ruffle looked good, 100 ruffles would make me a social success. She loved to sew and make me wear whatever came out of her machine. As a result, I went frilled and ruffled to ball games, funerals, scavenger hunts, Halloween parties (the only place my outfit was appropriate), and anywhere else I was invited.

In all the family album snapshots, I am beruffled, beribboned, and usually bedraggled. But during adolescence, I was too bewitched, bothered, and bewildered to protest or to even realize I was suffering from ruffle overload. And, since I knew nothing about psychiatry, I also had no idea that such a frilling experience should be ruining my psyche and giving me an ingrained terror of anything puckered (like those little lines that have appeared around my eyes recently).

On the other extreme, when my son reached the teen emergency zone, he always looked like he just crawled out of a clothes-for-the-needy donation box. If I was the victim of overdress, he made up for it by sinking to the depths of underdress.

His idea of style was ragged shorts, sloppy shirts, and one pair of shoes he wore *everywhere*—from church to overnight cave exploring. He would spend an hour in the shower and then step out to look through a pile of rumpled clothes on the floor to find something bad enough for the outfit of the day.

When it came to our experience of fashion, there was definitely a generation gap. But there were other gaps, too.

When I was a teen, our music was loud enough to make our parents complain but not loud enough to cause permanent hearing damage. We worried a lot but not about getting mugged or endangering the planet by using up all our natural resources, not about nuclear fallout or the air and water being polluted or contaminated. Since we come from two "different worlds," is it any wonder the generations have difficulty with dialogue, communication, and understanding?

But then I guess all generations have suffered from gap-itis and have survived. They say failure is the line of least persistence—so we must keep trying to close the gap and not get too tuckered out by that persistent pucker!

Dear Lord, maybe it's too bad we parents haven't had the kinds of experiences our children have had—to learn about other cultures, to engage in social-action projects, to travel more (either in person or by the TV screen), to communicate by computer. But Lord, maybe it's too bad our children haven't had the experiences we had—of more discipline and safety and innocence. Help us, Lord, to throw away our brooms that try to sweep away each other's likes and opinions. Help us to appreciate each other and to enjoy and learn from our "different worlds." And thank you, Lord, for such a frilling opportunity!

If the Shoe Fits...

L ast week, I did not put my best foot forward when I went to church.

Running late as usual, I was still shoeless when my husband honked the horn impatiently. I grabbed my black pumps from the closet, stepped into them, and dashed for the car. We were lucky to get a good parking spot so it was just a few steps to the door, and it wasn't until the middle of the service that I glanced down and noticed that there was something peculiar about my shoes.

Since I frequently wear black (hoping to look thin but only succeeding in looking funereal), I have two pairs of black pumps. One pair has medium heels and a little bow; the other pair has slightly higher heels and no bow. Last Sunday, I wore one of each.

Once again, I had put my foot into it.

I tried to hide my mismatched shoe by putting one foot behind the other. I tried to concentrate on the sermon, but the message got lost somewhere in the embarrassment. I kept thinking that soon it would be time to leave and there I'd go in the uneven heels, hippity-hopping down the aisle—and it wasn't even Easter.

Piously keeping my eyes downcast, I cut my eyes back and forth, trying to sneak a peak and see if anyone was snickering behind a song book. That's when I noticed the lady across the aisle with her head buried in her hands, deep in prayer, obviously troubled by some problem and seeking help.

Next my eye caught sight of a little boy on the other side. He had taken a seashell out of his pocket and was studying it as though it held a magic secret. Maybe it did. He may have missed some of the sermon (like I did), but he was getting a lasting lesson in the mysteries and wonders of nature.

Just then a baby cooed and laughed, and I looked around and saw the young father pick up the baby tenderly, patting his back, smiling at him lovingly. That father's face held a prayer of joy and gratitude.

Too late I realized that to those people—and to others who were using their time and thoughts *wisely*—my mismatched shoes were of little concern. And if there were some who had been looking idly around like I had been, well, maybe they *needed* a good laugh to help ease a week of life's everyday tensions.

Like so many of my problems, that absent-minded lapse was only important to *me* and, whether or not *anybody* noticed, it really wouldn't change the course of world history *or* church history.

In spite of that lesson learned, instead of stopping to visit outside church, I hippity-hopped out to the car as fast as my mismatched heels would carry me. I didn't mind giving folks one good laugh, but I wasn't bold enough to provide an encore.

Dear Lord, I hope I will remember those shoes the next time I get worried all out of shape about the fact that my dress is wrinkled all out of shape or my hair is all out of curl or my outfit is all out of style. Who cares what I wear—as long as it is clean and makes me look ten pounds thinner. Just kidding, Lord. I will try to worry less about the outside and more about the inside. And when I hear the story about the lilies of the field, I will remember, "If the shoe fits...."

Forgotten Treasures— Tut, Tut!

I know just how those explorers felt when they discovered King Tut's tomb. They peered inside and saw treasures—but also strange artifacts that had been buried so long nobody remembered what they once had been. That's how I feel when I look inside my refrigerator.

Whenever I have a case of the hungries, *everything* looks like a treasure—yesterday's leftover spaghetti, the last piece of meatloaf, the few spoonfuls of frozen yogurt in the bottom of the carton. Even the cottage cheese looks good.

But when I start sorting through the little plastic containers and foil-wrapped packages, I sometimes discover strange artifacts buried too long. Just recently I had a really revolting refrigerator experience.

I had invited friends over to play bridge and had made a fancy cheese ball and some nice snacks. A few minutes before they were due to arrive, a neighbor called asking me to run an urgent errand for her. I dashed out, telling my husband to greet the guests and tell them I would be back soon.

By the time I returned home, my bridge friends knew more about me and my refrigerator than I really wanted them to know.

They had decided to be "helpful" and get out the snacks for me. They had overlooked the fresh cheese ball, the thin-sliced salami, the dip, and veggies. They had rummaged around in the back somewhere amid the mystery packages and discovered three small chunks of moldy cheese and a sack of kumquats gone bad!

Now I know that not too many people have good *or* bad kumquats in their refrigerator, but I had bought some to go around the Christmas turkey because my mother always did that—and then of course I had forgotten them for a month. After all, what do you do with a leftover kumquat?

Dear Lord, today I've been thinking about my refrigerator and King Tut and kumquats and it occurred to me that relationships are like refrigerators. If you leave something on the shelf too long, it goes bad. If you neglect a marriage or a child or a friend or a relative, by the time you get back to paying attention, it may be too late. Help me, Lord, to be more alert and attentive. With today's hectic pace, it's easy to forget that you have to keep working on a marriage for it to work. It's easy to get too busy to listen to a child's small problem before it has a chance to grow into a large problem. It's easy to get too involved to find time for a friend or a relative. Help me, Lord, to be more careful with my treasures.

If the Hat Fits, Put It on and Pull It Down Over Your Ears

Today, I keep thinking about that country music legend, Minnie Pearl. I realize I should be thinking about toxic waste, world peace, or spiritual renewal. But I keep thinking about Minnie—and how she always wore a straw hat with a price tag dangling dizzily from the brim.

Last week, on one of my too-many moments of shopping madness, I just couldn't resist taking home a *darling* straw hat I saw on sale. Then on Sunday, when springtime filled the air and spring fever filled my head, I decided to really dress up and wear my new hat to church.

When I was all gussied up and ready to sail forth into the world, I looked into the mirror and knew that this was the kind of hat that would turn heads. Since so few people wear hats to church today, *any* kind of hat would turn heads, but I ignored that fact.

Just as I was about to go out the door, I got so carried away with my new look that I picked up a mirror from the dresser and twirled around to see how fabulous my new chapeau looked from the rear. Normally, I never look into my bedroom rearview mirror because I'm afraid I won't like the view. And besides, my personal philosophy is to look ahead, never back. But that once, I looked back and saw that—you guessed it—dangling from the darling hat was the price tag!

If only I hadn't looked back, everybody in church could have gotten a good laugh. As it was, I removed the tag from the hat but couldn't seem to remove the snicker from my face. All through the morning, all I could think of was me and Minnie Pearl.

Dear Lord, I think that every time in the next few weeks when I start to feel a little puffed up and ready to give myself a proud pat on the back, my high-hat attitude will dissolve into a vision of that high-hat price tag. But, like always, I will forget, Lord. When I do, remind me again of how fine the line is between fabulous and foolish, outstanding and outlandish, remarkable and ridiculous. When I start to prance and preen, tell me to check the rearview mirror. And thanks, Lord, for such a silly lesson. The tag is gone, but I still can't wipe that snicker off my face.

Family Secrets

What are the secrets of the universe? Ask any mother and she can tell you a few. I could tell you about the Inflection/Reflection Reaction or the Telephone Transcendental Meditation Maneuver or many others.

You probably already know about the I.R.R. That's when an out-of-sight kid suddenly lets out a scream loud enough to turn the air purple. His mother never even flinches. She just goes right on cleaning the oven, inventing a cure for the common jelly stain, or stitching up a crocodile costume for the school play. That's because the kid's *inflection* is wrong.

Another time that same kid can let out a similar scream and the mother will be instantly in air, dropping everything to dash frantically to the scene of the scream—and to the rescue!

Evidently a mother's reaction depends on something like that high-pitched whistle that can be heard only by dogs, not by folks. The emergency child-sound can be heard only by mothers, not by innocent bystanders. Our "trained" ears reflect on the inflection and instantly detect the difference between a momentary frustration or irritation and a genuine *red alert*.

Now the Telephone Transcendental Meditation Maneuver is another very popular one. Any mother will tell you that the minute she gets on the telephone, a child will suddenly appear at her elbow. The house can be deserted when she picks up the phone but somehow, within seconds, a child will appear from nowhere to tug at Mommy and whine loudly for immediate attention.

That child could have been next door or down the block or in a soundproof room busily drawing a detailed picture of a nuclear bomb for show-and-tell. No problem. The minute Mommy got on the phone and started to explain to the Electric Company that the computer must have made a mistake because a family of four could not possibly use enough electricity in one month to get a bill for three million dollars—that's the minute the child's transcendental telepathy will tell him or her to hurry to Mommy's side for whine time.

But I have also discovered a lesser-known secret of the universe. It seems that even children who no longer live at home know exactly the *wrong* minute to communicate with a parent.

My friends and I agree that the minute we are dashing out the door to go to an important meeting, a party, or a dentist appointment, the phone will ring. It will be a married daughter or a college-age son who has suddenly decided it is time for a nice friendly chat with the folks. We may not have heard from that child for weeks and we may be hungry for news and conversation, but the *only* time an "away" child will be in the mood to talk is at the moment Mom or Dad is hurrying out the door—and running late.

It seems that children never outgrow Telephone Telepathy.

Dear Lord, thank you for telephones and children who call. It must have been awful for the pioneers whose children left in covered wagons and could only communicate with them via Pony Express. But Lord, it does seem that when you built in that telepathy you could have used a little better timing device.

The Trash Man Cometh

If anyone ever asked me to submit a list of my "ten most-admired people," do you know who I would have to include? My garbage man!

I realize that garbage collector is not exactly one of the most coveted jobs in the world, but he does his work with pride and efficiency and—believe it or not—with courtesy and cheerfulness. How many executives can make that statement?

Now this young man does not look like what you might envision the driver of a garbage truck. His blond good looks would make him eligible to appear in one of the ads you see in magazines or on TV—advertising ski clothing, soft drinks, or any "fun" product. Dressed appropriately, he could mingle at any cocktail party and look like the typical young "comer" on his way up. No one would ever guess that trash is his business.

Usually he works alone, but some days he has a helper who lolls along, halfheartedly picking up cans. It's obvious that our hero does twice the work in half the time. He has his job down to a science, a symphony of movement, timed to make each step count. And yet he is not so tied to his routine that he can't take time to help.

If neighbors are a bit late putting out the trash and he sees them scurrying toward the curb, he doesn't drive off in a huff, reminding them to be on time next week. Instead, he strides up the driveway to take the cans from them and answers apologies with a pleasant "no problem." So you see why his name would have to be on my "admired" list.

In today's comfort-oriented society, even those with cushy, well-paid jobs sometimes complain about their "miserable" working conditions. And some employees who are supposed to serve the public—in supermarkets, department stores, restaurants—seem insulted if you ask them for any extras. When you call an office for information, you often get surly replies, are transferred from one uninformed employee to another, and then get cut off and have to start all over.

Yet my trash collector continues in his courteous, efficient manner—and even offers a bit of philosophy.

One day I had chopped down half a rose bush and had the prickly branches in a pile at the curb. When I heard the rumble of the garbage truck, I dashed out, wearing long sleeves and heavy gloves to protect my arms from the thorns, planning to toss the branches in the truck while Mr. Wonderful emptied the trash cans. But he would have none of it, insisting that he would take care of the branches for me. I cautioned, "Watch out for those thorns—they stick to your clothes." He answered, "Yeah—they're just like love; once they get hold of you, they won't let go."

There are a lot of people who could take lessons from my garbage man. Maybe we *all* could.

✙

Dear Lord, work may be a four-letter word, but it doesn't have to be a dirty one. The next time I have a dirty or difficult job to do, remind me to make the best of it instead of whining, procrastinating, and acting like a poor pitiful victim. And the next time I'm down in the dumps, help me to remember the inspiring example of my trash man—so I can get up and get off my can!

Whose Label Are You Wearing Today?

Every time I go to the post office, I feel like a loose woman. They have all these mailboxes marked for Bulk, Bundles, Express, etc.—and then there's the box for Loose Letters. Now although I don't write loose letters, my mail is never important enough to be bundled or expressed, so I have no choice but to head for the box labeled "Loose."

Every time I go to the grocery, I feel like a slow woman. No matter how lean my list is, I never seem to have few enough items to get into the fast lane, so I have no choice but to head for the slow lane.

Every time I go to the gas station, I feel like a self-serving woman. I was taught it is not nice to be self-serving, but what can I do? The only way to save a few pennies is to bypass the full-service pump and head for the one labeled "Self-Service."

Yes, labels can be limiting and misleading. Some people get labeled in childhood and grow up thinking they are not as smart or as attractive as others. Some get a super-critical boss on a first job and spend a career wearing an interior label of inferiority, always on the defensive, always expecting to be corrected or belittled.

For some, a label spells defeat. For others, it becomes a challenge to excel somewhere, somehow—to prove something to the world and to themselves.

But there's one good thing about a label—it can always be changed. Some people change a life label by moving to a new town and a new environment. Some do it by going back to school to learn a new profession or trade or craft. Some make the change by switching on the power of positive thinking.

However, I don't think the post office, grocery, or gas station will change their labels—so I guess that means I am stuck with being a loose, slow, self-serving woman.

Dear Lord, forgive my foolishness. I know how important it is to ignore labels, to rise above and grow beyond. Lord, I know that some people have given *you* a label, too. Some think of you as a harsh taskmaster who must be feared and addressed only in the formal surroundings of a church. Others think of you as all smiles and alleluias and forget about commandments to be obeyed as a way of life. How sad, Lord, to try to limit you when you are limitless, to label you when you are infinite. Thank you, Lord for being a personal friend and at the same time incomprehensible— always beckoning me to delve deeper into your mystery and majesty. Thank you, Lord, for the wonder and yet the warmth, for the unknown and yet the knowing. And help me to remember, Lord, that the only label I should ever wear is the one that says, "Made by God."

Dancing in the Rain

I've been seeing the world through gold-colored glasses. I know, I know. It's supposed to be rose-colored glasses, but I never get things quite right.

This all started when a friend went to Florida and brought me some wraparound plastic sunglasses that had two benefits: They cut out all the damaging rays hiding in that glorious summertime brightness *and* I could put them on over my reading glasses and see to read in the sunshine.

They were exciting, too, because they made me look like all I needed was a pilot's cap and a white scarf and I would be ready to take off into the wild blue. The color of the glasses was also a wild blue. And that was a problem.

Those blue glasses made everything in the world look blue. Even on a bright, golden day, they made the view blue and somber. All the brilliant red and pink flowers took on a funereal purple glow. And the sunshine just faded into the blue.

I tried to wear them to keep out the rays, but I desperately wanted to let in the glow. Then one day I was at our friendly neighborhood pharmacy and there was a similar pair of glasses, but instead of blue, they were a bright golden yellow. Just for instance, I tried them on and—hello!—it was a go for the glow! They lit up my life!

When I got home, I took the glasses and a book to the patio. As I glanced around, the flowers seemed cheerier, the trees looked

brighter, and my psyche got perkier. I settled back to enjoy the balmy sunny day. When read time was up, I took a last look around at the lovely sunniness and then took off the glasses to go inside.

What a shock! Bare-eyed, I realized that the sun was long gone, the sky was totally overcast, and gray clouds were rolling in so fast that by the time I raced into the house, sheets of rain were pelting the patio. I put the glasses back on, and even in the middle of the storm, my garden was sunny!

After that, I knew just what to do when things looked blue—just look at the world through my gold-colored glasses.

Dear Lord, I guess most things in my world can be shaded and colored by my attitude, my way of looking at things. When I have a blue view, even good news can seem bad. But when I have a sunny outlook, I can see that bad news is never totally dark or hopeless. Help me, Lord, to remember that all through history, people have survived and learned from mistakes. Pitfalls have often brought about progress, and arguments have resulted in agreements. I know it takes prayer and work to make such things happen, but it also takes a *be*-attitude. Help me, Lord, to be ever hopeful. Help me to keep my sunny side up.

Apple-Bobbing

If an apple a day keeps the doctor away, I could have dropped my health insurance this year.

When we moved into this house, a scraggly little apple tree was growing out by the patio and a tree "expert" told me I might as well chop it down unless I just wanted shade because it would never have an apple on it. For some unknown reason, the former owners of the house had sawed off the top of the main trunk of the tree and all the branches were suckers, growing out of the sides in an unmannerly fashion.

Well, I *did* want shade and besides, I liked the little sucker! So I did not chop down the apple tree. It stayed by our patio and quietly grew and cast a bit more shade each year. Then one springtime, it rewarded us for our friendship. We looked out the window one morning and saw a picture-perfect tree totally covered with a froth of fluffy, white apple blossoms. We reveled in the beauty while it lasted and wondered if the blossoms would turn into apples. In the fall, there were three little apples on the tree.

Since then, each springtime the tree has put on a show of incredible beauty, and each fall it has produced a few inedible apples. But this year was different.

Another "expert" came by and said we better get all our trees sprayed to protect them against the effects of this year's drought and the dread diseases sure to follow. So the apple tree got sprayed

along with the others. And this was just what it had been waiting for. Suddenly we had a bushel and a peck of apples—plus a lesson to be learned.

As I picked and peeled those apples, I began to think of how some people are like our apple tree. Even though they've been "stunted," sawed off by lack of education, money, or opportunity, they've still managed to flourish and give others whatever gifts they could muster—comforting shade, blossoming beauty, fruits of the spirit.

Yet others who have been given so much return so little. What a shame.

Dear Lord, thank you for the apple tree and all the apple pies we've been enjoying. I was surprised to find that some of the apples looked as pretty as a picture, but when I cut into them, they were rotten at the core. Others that looked kind of scruffy on the outside were perfect on the inside and absolutely delicious. Help me to remember that, Lord, when I watch TV and see all the glittery, beautiful lifestyles and start to hunger and yearn for what I don't have and forget to be glad for what I do have. And on those days, Lord, when I'm struggling on rocky ground and feel like a sucker, remind me that, like the apple tree, I can still bloom where I was planted.

Driving Me Crazy

Recently my all-grown-up, six-foot-tall handsome son moved back to our hometown, and he often shows up at my house for dinner. During these visits, he has been checking me out for the signs of advanced old age.

One day he said to me, "Mom, you're getting too old to drive at night. You really should not do that any more." I didn't tell him that I am the designated driver for several friends who expect me to pick them up for meetings, church suppers, and various after-dark get-togethers. I just changed the subject, passed the potatoes, and hoped this phase would pass. It did.

A couple of weeks later, he casually said, "Mom, I'll be out of town on a business trip for a few days next week, but I'll be back Friday night. Could you pick me up at the airport? My plane gets in around midnight."

Being the wonderful mother that I am, I did not mention that midnight comes after dark.

Since then, he has been on many business trips that usually end on Friday night, and his old mother has been at the airport, waiting to give him a ride home—always after dark.

Dear Lord, I am so happy that my son lives nearby now, after a lot of years when his work meant living in another part of the country. He is so much fun to be with, and his conversations challenge me to consider new ideas and possibilities. I'm not sure if this is keeping me young or aging me faster, but it is interesting and I really don't mind mingling with the sparse midnight traffic at the airport. Sometimes I wait in the cell-phone parking lot until his flight arrives. Other times I park and go into the terminal to sit and have fun people-watching while waiting. Either way I enjoy the conversation riding home, hearing about his week and rejoicing that I can still be out in your wonderful world—after dark.

Pagan Is
as Pagan Does

My cat is a pagan. He never goes to church. He looks at my husband and meows in a tone that is obviously cat-cuss. And he is suspected of swiping food from the dish of the cat next door, whose owners provide him with the kind of expensive gourmet goodies that are not to be found in the cat dish at our house.

In spite of all his terrible sins, this cat definitely acts like a Christian at times. He comforts the lonely. He will jump into any empty lap to purr and befriend anyone who seems forlorn or lonely (obviously not realizing that cats are supposed to be aloof and a bit uppity).

He has faith and trust. As soon as he determines you're open to friendship, he rolls over on his back in a totally vulnerable position to invite you to scratch his tummy—and when you do, he looks at you adoringly, mutely telling you that no matter what the world says, he thinks you are a wonderful person.

And he visits the poor: He spends time with me every day!

Even though this cat has some obvious character flaws, he spreads cheer and consolation. And he never makes you feel abandoned because he has to hurry off to some important appointment. If you need a friend, he'll stick around all day.

Today it's not easy to find someone who is not too busy to sit and visit with a friend who needs comfort or lay in the grass with a child who needs company. Everyone is working around the clock to accumulate things. We live in a world where everything has a high price tag, and you have to work extra hard or do without. There's little time left to comfort and counsel, to notice the needs of family and friends. Are we "doing without" the important things? Are we paying too high a price? Is it my cat who is the pagan?

Dear Lord, today it seems people are constantly working to earn money or status, evidently thinking this is more important than taking time out for a hug or a lazy afternoon listening to each other. Some even see older parents and relatives as a bother when they expect their children to take time out from their busy schedule to show up for family dinners or get-togethers. Forgive us, Lord, when we put work before family—and before *you*. Forgive us for thinking that work is more important than prayer, that this world is more important than the next. Help us to realize that even the busiest person needs a day of rest. *You* took one, Lord. You created the whole world and then took the seventh day off. Even then you were teaching us a lesson, weren't you, Lord? Well, I've learned my lesson, so I have to go now, Lord. It's time for me to take a nap with my nonpagan cat.

Give Me a Hand

One day I was busy cooking dinner and couldn't open a new twist-top of a jar that I needed to add to the recipe. Usually I would look in my junk drawer and find the "gripper" that helps me open things, but my son was standing by the counter, so I said, "Could you open this for me?" He gave it a good twist and it opened easily, of course. Then he looked at his poor aging mother and said, "Your hands are getting really weak, aren't they?"

I did not mention they were strong enough to drag in all the groceries needed to cook supper and strong enough to lift the big pans needed to cook those groceries. I just got a grip on myself and resolved I would always have my gripper handy if I needed to open anything.

The next night, I was leaving to pick up someone and go to the bridge club. My son, the newly appointed aging expert, said, "You still play bridge? Are your hands strong enough to shuffle the cards?"

I shuffled out to the car that is not supposed to leave the house after dark and gripped the steering wheel so tightly I almost did a "U-eeeee" pulling out of the driveway.

Dear Lord, I know my son means well and thinks he's looking out for me as I fade fast. Maybe he is just trying to adjust to the fact that I am a lot older than I was the last time he lived in the same town I do, and maybe I am not the do-everything Mighty Mom he remembers. I am also having a hard time trying to adjust to being a less Super Mom. So Lord, help me think of some snappy comebacks when he says things like, "You know, your hair would look a lot better *all* gray instead of half-and-half." I can't keep gritting my teeth to say nothing because the gritting might break off some of my aging teeth, and I would need more than my gripper to twist a dentist's bill into my budget.

Me and My Portulaca

There is a portulaca on my porch—and it is a pretty particular plant. As evening slowly creeps in, the portulaca slowly curls itself up into tiny little bud bundles and goes to sleep for the night. In the morning, it is not an early riser. It waits until about 10 o'clock when the sun comes around the corner of the house, and that is like a warm wake-up call. The portulaca yawns, shakes itself, and bursts into a profusion of pink, orange, red, and white flowers, forming a smashingly beautiful bouquet. *But* if a cloud appears in the afternoon, the portulaca must think it's time for an afternoon nap because it curls itself up again and looks like a bundle of teeny tiny green blankets just when my neighbor comes by to see the profusely blooming plant I've been bragging about.

Oh yes! Just when I no longer have any kids living at my house, I have adopted a plant that acts like the way my kid used to do—curling up into a don't-speak-to-me mood just when I wanted to show off how handsome, charming, and intelligent he was.

And, although I never thought cheery-deary me could have anything in common with a portulaca myself, maybe I do, too. I am not a morning person. I wake up slowly, get a cup of tea or coffee, meditate and meander, trying to remember where I'm supposed to be when, and check my calendar to be sure I haven't forgotten anything important. But once the sunshine peeks in my window, I also blossom forth and hit the road. I may not blossom as much as I once did and I may nap a bit more, but this garden of life is still so full of the joy of a home with a porch and portulacas and always new portals waiting to be opened.

Dear Lord, the portulaca and I thank you for the sunshine and for being planted in a friendly spot. I promise to try to do more praying and meditating as I meander—ever rejoicing in the wonder of your world. Thanks for letting me be a part of it.

Shoo, Fly!

There's a fly in my ointment! For years, I only drank black coffee, but recently I have returned to my youthful choice of cream *and* sugar. So now I sit down with a cup of coffee and am enjoying my morning ointment when I am summoned—the doorbell, the oven bell, the washer or dryer buzzer, or the phone seek my attention. So I put down the coffee cup. By the time I get back to it, there is often a fly floating in it, evidently having fallen to the temptation of cream and sugar. Maybe I should learn from this to find a better fly-catching method.

Now unfortunately, my work ethic seems to have also returned to my youthful practices. I know I should clear out that closet and although I have an afternoon appointment, the morning has some free time so I start vigorously to clean out, throw out, rearrange—and then temptation lurks. I remember I got that new book from the library yesterday and my urge to clean is ebbing so I think it's time for a little rest and I will just put my feet up and read one chapter. Then, of course, like the fly, I am lured to read one more chapter and one more, and soon it is time to get ready for the afternoon appointment and the closet stuff is now in a messy pile on the bedroom floor.

I have got to quit returning to my slovenly youthful ways. Old age is supposed to make me wiser, but that cream and sugar tastes so good, and it's always been hard for me to resist the lure of a new unread book. Well, I don't have time to worry about that now. I've got to clean out the cream and sugar and fly from my coffee cup before I put it in my blessedly electric dishwasher. Now if I could just find an electric closet-cleaner, maybe I would have more time for reading so I could get older *and* wiser.

Dear Lord, why is it that as I age, I can easily return to my foolish youthful habits but not to the good ones? Oh, maybe I didn't have any good ones. Hmmm, I better pray about that.

A Dream Come True

I noticed there was an empty lot across the street from the entrance to my subdivision, but I never paid much attention *until* the day I saw it was filled with piles of construction material. After that, every weekend, a man—sometimes alone, sometimes with friends—would be there constructing. It was just a small lot so I figured it would have to be a very modest house. But as I kept watching, I was happily surprised to see it grow *up* as well as across and, after a few months of start-and-stop work, it slowly turned into a lovely, well-planned, two-story home.

There were interesting stone corners on the brick, a two-peaked roof, a two-car garage, and a deck in the back that faced a grouping of trees that had been there maybe for years, just waiting for someone to come along and enjoy them. As the house snuggled in, the lot didn't look small anymore. It looked just right.

One day as I was driving past, I spotted the new owner and his wife outside watering the newly planted bushes. They looked surprised when this stranger pulled into the driveway, jumped out of the car, and rushed over to them. I said, "I just had to stop to congratulate you. I live in the neighborhood and I've watched your home grow and go up and it is sooo beautiful. It has truly been an inspiration to see you do it all on your own. It's the first 'handmade house' I've ever seen." The owner then beamed with a huge smile and said, "Thanks a lot for saying that. Ever since I was a kid, I always wished and hoped that I could some day build my own house. It took a lot of work and a lot of time and a lot of help from friends, but at last, it's my dream come true."

Dear Lord, many people have a wish, a hope, to someday become a billionaire, fly to the moon, travel to exotic places, play a perfect golf game, or make a perfect pie crust. Some few, like my neighbor and me, are lucky—and blessed.

As you know, Lord, since I was a kid my wish was to become a writer. You may have noticed that I kept working toward it—taking writing courses, reading other writers' works, sending off articles or book proposals that got rejected. I finally got jobs or freelance work, writing radio and TV commercials, catalog copy, magazine articles, whatever.

But, with your help, Lord, my first book was finally published when I was fifty years old. Since then, I've been lucky to have one or two books published almost every year, wrote my own national newspaper column for a number of years, and had lots of autograph parties where I happily got to meet the folks who read my scribblings.

Thank you, Lord, for so many blessings. I know there are many who have dreams that do not come true, and many, like me, who are grateful some of their young and foolish dreams did *not* come true. So thank you, Lord, for dreams and dreamers—when dreams come true and sometimes even when they don't.

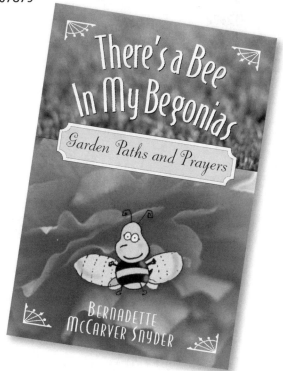

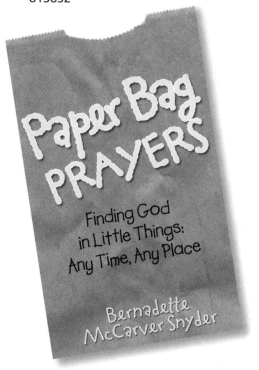

Graham Crackers, Galoshes and God: Every Woman's Book of Cope and Hope

144-page paperback

$11.99

437788